QUARTERBACK
DAD

Bobby Mercer with
Alison D. Schonwald, MD, FAAP

— A —
PLAY-BY-PLAY
GUIDE TO TACKLING
YOUR NEW BABY

adamsmedia
avon, massachusetts

Published by
Adams Media, an F+W Publications Company
57 Littlefield Street, Avon, MA 02322. U.S.A.
www.adamsmedia.com

ISBN-13: 978-1-59869-526-7
ISBN-10: 1-59869-526-6

Printed in the United States of America.

J I H G F E D C B A

Library of Congress Cataloging-in-Publication Data
is available from the publisher.

This publication is designed to provide accurate and authoritative
information with regard to the subject matter covered. It is sold with
the understanding that the publisher is not engaged in rendering
legal, accounting, or other professional advice. If legal advice or
other expert assistance is required, the services of a competent
professional person should be sought.
—From a *Declaration of Principles* jointly adopted by
a Committee of the American Bar Association and a
Committee of Publishers and Associations

Many of the designations used by manufacturers and sellers to
distinguish their product are claimed as trademarks. Where those
designations appear in this book and Adams Media was aware of
a trademark claim, the designations have been printed with initial
capital letters.

Interior illustrations by Eric Andrews.

This book is available at quantity discounts for bulk purchases.
For information, please call 1-800-289-0963.

To Nicole—
my own Rookie of the Year

Contents

ACKNOWLEDGMENTS

Watching thirty-five kids come together to win a state championship was an unbelievable thrill, but it paled in comparison to the birth of my daughter. I'd like to thank my Rookie of the Year for being sweet, good-natured, and understanding when her QB dad takes too long to get a bottle of breast milk.

I have the best head coach in the business, my wife Michele. Your support, love, and friendship make our team run smoothly. You definitely win my Coach of the Year trophy.

I wish to thank our parents—Buzz, Joyce, Richard, and Nancy—for providing us great role models for keeping relationships together and healthy.

Books don't happen without the support of many people. I wish to thank my agent, Kathy Green, for her help, guidance, and championing of this book. I want to thank Andrea Norville, Meredith O'Hayre, and the wonderful people at Adams Media for believing in this book and lending their expertise.

I want to thank all of my great friends for listening and offering anecdotes. Thanks to Jeff Andrews, Scott Buchanan, David Burdette, Rich Canamucio, Dana and Kim Conner, Matt Daigle, Mike Flowe, Richard Gabriel, Mike Garity, Gene Hammonds, Kim Kessler, Matt Kissling, Mitch Leonard, Charlie Metcalf, Joe Potter, Courtney Ross, Bill Silver, Marvin Smith, April Spencer, Bill Van Cleve, Rex Wells, and Danny Wilkins.

A special thanks to all the coaches I have worked with over the years who put family first. The lessons I learned from you were more important than any Xs and Os.

INTRODUCTION

From the time you are born, you learn about sports—the games, the rules, the playbook. Teachers and coaches drill you on the finer points of your particular sport, assuring you that if you play by the rules you will succeed. A good player always succeeds. Picture yourself grown up, standing in the delivery room as your child is born and carefully handed to you. During that first moment of wonder, you feel the fear of a new parent—what are you supposed to do with this new human? What are the rules? Where is the playbook?! With all the babies born last year, not a single one came with a playbook, leaving many new fathers on the sidelines trying to figure out how best to get into this game.

Football is the ultimate team sport played by the ultimate team athletes. In no other team sport do so many players all have individual tasks that must be done well to succeed. Just like winning in football, raising great kids is a goal of all new dads, and there are individual tasks that need to be done to accomplish that goal.

Taking a lighthearted approach to fatherhood, this book approaches the phases of becoming a father as though they were part of a typical football season, with need-to-know advice sprinkled throughout. As a twenty-year coach of the most popular sport in America, I learned many of the skills necessary to help mold a successful team: organizational skills; the ability to talk to people; the ability to cajole, persuade, and even dissuade kids from certain behaviors; and the importance of planning. The transition to being a dad became easier when I realized the same skills needed for having and raising a baby were those I had already learned through football. This book will help many dads learn these same skills. It will be like your mom hiding medicine in your pudding when you were a kid. Guys want to be good dads; they just need a little help. This book will be your guide. It is divided into two halves:

1. PREGAME

Most likely, finding out that your partner is pregnant is going to be a surprise. You have just signed a twenty-plus-year contract with a new team, a team consisting of three or more teammates. This section covers all of the impending fatherhood issues like the initial reaction, choosing a name, equipment issues, money matters, and getting to the hospital. The thrill of having a new prospect in the house will surpass the thrill of any approaching football season.

The drive to the hospital and the delivery is a frenzied joy ride equal to any USC versus UCLA football game. As frantic as this time might be, take a few minutes to prepare for the game and enjoy it. Just like packing for a tailgate party, plan ahead. The thrill of being handed your own first-round draft pick is a moment that you will cherish forever.

2. GAME DAY

Once your star is here you start game day. No game day is complete without a plan. Learn how to schedule your time to make all of your game days more memorable. Just like coaching a big game, duties and responsibilities need to be shared among all the members of the team. As the QB dad, you will take a larger role in the household. Roll up your sleeves and prepare for one of the best years of your life. The first year is crucial in the development of your little prospect and establishing a lasting bond. Call upon the wisdom of experts to help you. At the end of the first year, sit back and celebrate all the successes. Tips for throwing a memorable Super Bowl party and hints for the future will be given.

I have a wonderful child, and the first year was one of joy and frustration. I refer to my daughter throughout this book, but the advice can apply for both girls and boys. I am not an expert by any means, just a guy with a new daughter. Follow the advice set forth by the doctors.

This book is designed to give you a look at what the future holds for the next eighteen months of your life. I'll frequently give you tips to help you along in your growth as a dad.

Touchdown

Touchdowns are tips that will help make you a better dad.

Fumbles are humorous things about fatherhood, or things that you should never do.
Fumble

NFLs (New Football Language) are football terms that will take on a completely new meaning once you have a child in the house. For example a **tight end** *is when your baby is constipated.*

Playbook pages are graphics that will summarize some of the most important hints on many topics. Extra Points are added reminders of some of the important advice given in each chapter. The most important advice that any new dad can get is this: You only get one chance to raise your kids.

Part 1

PREGAME

1. A BLUE-CHIP PROSPECT

The first time you hear you are going to be a father you will experience a range of emotions. Your first emotion is going to be a gut feeling, whether fear, joy, or a little of both. This is like finding out who your favorite team selected on draft day. It is okay to be scared; that is a common reaction. When I found out my wife was expecting, I had an initial wave of elation soon followed by the feeling of impending responsibility. I literally felt myself grow up (for a few minutes, anyway). Whatever your initial feelings are, nobody has to know but you. Chances are your teammate is feeling many of the same emotions. If your initial thought is anger, it is probably a good idea to never tell your teammate. First reactions are sometimes just wrong. Remember, the Eagle fans booed Donovan McNabb on draft day.

WHAT DOES THAT PINK LINE MEAN ANYWAY?

You have just seen the pink or blue line for the first time. Your brain is flooded with a rainbow of emotions: sheer joy, elation, fear, love, and downright terror. What do you do now? Imagine yourself coaching her team to the champion-ship game? Picture yourself watching with fascination as she takes her first teetering steps? Look forward to hours of play-ing with her Playstation 6 or Xbox 720 and letting her win occasionally (but never at sports games)? Try not to think about hiding the car keys when she turns sixteen and prom dates from hell? What have you gotten yourself into?

I remember how I felt when I found out my teammate was expecting. We had friends over and were going to go out to eat when she got home from work. Right before we left for dinner, my teammate asked me to come into the bedroom for a moment. She held up a plastic pregnancy test and asked me if I knew what the pink lines meant. My brain spun like a frat boy during rush week. I hugged her as my mind raced. Then we went out to eat and made small talk as if nothing had changed. Our life was about to be turned upside down and we were sitting there pretending everything was normal, talking about upcoming games and mutual friends. As we sat at dinner, the thought of being a dad sunk in and I became truly giddy about having a baby.

Your life is about to be changed forever because of two simple pastel lines. Why do the lines (or plus signs) have to be pastel colored anyway? Is it society's first attempt to minimize the importance of guys in the birth process? Guys would be much happier with Clemson orange, Raider black, or Gator blue lines. Guys are incredibly important in the birth pro-cess. After all, if not for us, a romantic dinner, and a bottle of wine, there might not be a baby.

Guys will always want the test repeated just to be sure. Even though I was happy with my teammate being pregnant,

I asked her if we ought to get an official doctor's test to be sure. She looked at me like I was an idiot. My teammate is a doctor (and she took the test at work). I went out that night and bought a home pregnancy test from the supermarket anyway. Four pink lines in twenty-four hours sealed the deal. I was going to be a dad. I really wanted to be sure before we told people—and you should too.

LETTING PEOPLE KNOW

When to tell people you're expecting a delivery from the stork may create a disagreement between you and the mom (the mom being the baby's mother. I'll refer to your mom as Grammy, Grandmom, Nana, Grandma, Ninny, and so on). How long should you wait to tell people? Many people wait twelve weeks because of fetal health concerns. You can consider this minicamp. With first kids, waiting can be especially difficult. It starts with a phone call to the teammate's parents and snowballs. Many grandmothers get more excited than mothers. They get a wonderful new child to spoil with a minimum amount of diaper changing responsibilities. I can hear Grammy now, "Oops, the baby smells . . . you better take care of that."

As you tell nonrelatives, you will get one of several reactions. The reaction will depend on whether your teammate is with you. If she is with you, you will cease to exist right after the word *pregnant* escapes your lips. Announcing a pregnancy is a woman's moment to shine. You might get a free beer (or free tickets) out of the announcement, but you will not get the same result as your teammate. If you don't like telling people in person, tell the ESPN insider in your circle of friends. Every circle has one person who freely shares the gossip, and if you tell them, it is better than an ad on the JumboTron.

 *Telling the **ESPN insider** is better than an ad on the JumboTron.*

If you are sans teammate, the reactions will depend on whether there are women present anyway. Women will congratulate you and hug you; they are truly happy for you as a couple. They will look at you as more of a man than a guy at this point. When you tell the guys, the reaction will be more muted. They are very happy for you as they now have less competition for the lake house, Ferrari, and Porsche, and you just might be willing to give them your spare tickets to the big game when you can't go.

 Getting congratulated for being pregnant is a foreign concept to all men before they have a child.

Like most guys, getting congratulated for being pregnant was a foreign concept to me. After all, I wasn't pregnant! Were they congratulating me because I boinked my teammate? I actually boink my teammate on a regular basis and enjoy it. It was still hard for me to say "we are pregnant" for months. That becomes easier to deal with and you will eventually get used to it. I imagine for a second child the congratulations get easier to accept. It still sounds silly when I hear people say it. But I now find myself congratulating male friends now that "they" are pregnant.

CONCEIVING THE HARD WAY

First of all, if you had difficulty conceiving, a standing ovation is in order now that your teammate is pregnant. You are going to have a baby and all of the fun that comes with it. All the serious things can come later; enjoy the moment.

If you and your partner had difficulty conceiving, then accept the congratulations with the deepest gratitude. My teammate and I got pregnant rather easily, and it was a lot of fun! My teammate can actually feel ovulation. We tried for all of four weeks before she got pregnant. My teammate is Italian-American Catholic, so I just really had to be in the same room with her.

 Struggling to conceive can lead you to be treated like a
Fumble *sex machine. Fumbles sometimes lead to a touchdown. Struggling to conceive also leads to extra reps in practice.*

We didn't have to chart days, take internal temperatures, read our horoscopes or tea leaves, or any other method of predicting ovulation. You can even buy kits that will predict the exact date. They must work because if you read the boxes they assure you these kits work. A woman's body temperature rises during the release of the egg, so your partner may take her temperature to track this. When her temp spikes, she puts on romantic music and you have to go to work. The good news is that sperm will be good for up to seventy-two hours inside her tubes; the egg is only good for about twenty-four hours. It is amazing that anybody gets pregnant. If you struggled to conceive, you understand what it is like to be treated like a sex machine. You have to perform on cue several days in a row. This has to remove some of the romance from your evening, even with the romantic music.

EARLY TRAINING CAMP WORRIES

There are some early concerns in the pregnancy game. The sex of your future star is definitely on your mind. Do you wish for a little boy that you can watch in a college football game someday or a little girl that you can spoil to death? Even though it is too early, you still will wonder and dream. You also may want to make a few temporary lifestyle choices in the next several months. For the first few weeks it will seem like you just won the Super Bowl. Enjoy those feelings.

Quarterback or Cheerleader

Wondering about the sex of your future superstar is going to eat up a lot of spare time in the coming months. Even if you want to know, you usually can't find out until sixteen to twenty weeks into the pregnancy. By the way, in today's age, pregnancies are measured in weeks, not months. Forty weeks is the standard that is used to predict due dates. Nine months is from the good old days, like when we were born.

You will spend hours dreaming about your future star, but don't get your heart set on one sex or the other. Nature is funny; it doesn't give you a choice, but many people try anyway. I had a friend who even went so far as to try certain positions and times of day to ensure the sex of his kid. He did get what he wanted, but I still think of it like calling the opening coin toss. He had a 50 percent chance of being right. Just focus on hoping the kid comes out healthy. Ten fingers, ten toes, and a healthy kid is all most people really want. Regardless of its standard equipment, the first time you look at that little baby you will love her!

Alcohol During Training Camp

Another thing to think about in the early stages of your teammate's pregnancy is the alcohol factor. You can sometimes figure out that a woman is pregnant if she chooses tonic with a twist instead of a beer at a tailgate party. The common recommendation is no alcohol for her after she finds out she has a bun in the oven, which is ironic since a few babies never would have been conceived without alcohol.

You have an important decision to make that will affect the next several months of your life. Do you give up alcohol for your partner's sake? Do you cut back in support of her? Or do you celebrate that you will have a designated driver for about the next year? Some women will have no problem if you continue to have a beer or four, but some will resent the fact that you still can have a drink while she won't be able to have any alcohol. If your partner doesn't mind you drinking, you now have a designated driver for a while. I chose to abstain to lend moral support to my teammate. The difficulty of this decision will be based on whether you only drink occasionally or if you like to have a few pretty much every day. I only slipped up twice during the pregnancy. Once was the night we found out because the news hadn't quite sunk in yet. The other was at midnight after a particularly adrenaline-draining football game as I sat with the other coaches and wives. My teammate took the car keys after only one beer.

If she breast-feeds, you may have to make a longer commitment (or you can get more free rides home). Breast-feeding moms need to avoid guzzling alcohol for a longer time frame, since it is bad for the baby. A glass of wine may be acceptable, but that will be her limit. Encourage her to breast-feed if she wants to breast-feed, and after the birth let her feel good about being a designated driver (by the way, it is great for the baby too).

CHANGING FROM GUY TO MAN

Guys are different than men. All males fall on a sliding scale from 100 percent guy to 100 percent man. A perfect QB dad has qualities of both: a fun side and a serious side.

Maybe having a kid makes you become a little bit more of a man, but your guy side will still be present. The guy side is that ten-year-old boy that lives in most males. It causes us to laugh when we fart and long for toys to play with. I think that most women secretly prefer guys to men. Some of your gal pals will appear to get hung up on the worst guys. Guys have a slight air of danger, similar to a mustang that has never been ridden. And almost all people (both sexes) like a challenge.

Fumble *You will have to learn how to balance being a guy and a man. Having a guy side will come in very handy as you progress toward the start of the regular season.*

The trick in fatherdom is to balance being a guy and a man. You are going to be responsible for raising a child with the woman you love, but remember that your partner most likely fell in love with the guy side of your personality. The guy side will come in very handy as you progress toward the start of the regular season. Guys just laugh more than men do. You are going to need the ability to laugh and roll with the punches as you head toward opening day.

WHAT TO LOOK FORWARD TO

Before I saw the pink lines, I imagined pregnancy, birth, and kid rearing to be kind of like a football season, a frantic rush of ups and downs with a few moments of terror. Most football seasons only last six or seven months. You just got signed for a twenty-year contract (or longer). Your season is starting and you haven't even flipped a coin for the first game yet. Well, hang on and enjoy the season.

The memories created with your little prospect will delight you for years to come. Her falling asleep on your chest during a big game, watching her try to walk in your shoes, and the first time she says "Da" will be unforgettable. Remember and cherish these moments, because in twelve years she is going to think you are the dumbest person alive.

Touchdown

 Girl or boy really doesn't matter; you now have a companion to go to games with or yell at the television screen with.

If your idea of a perfect weekend is high-school games on Friday, college games on Saturday, and pro games on Sunday, you are in for a treat. You're going to have a new blue-chip prospect in the house. You will soon have a partner to yell at the television with.

THE NEW TEAM

Your team is going to grow in the next forty weeks. Be prepared for a possible increased role in the day-to-day activities of life. As the QB dad, you have many varied and new responsibilities.

Your future star will go from undrafted free agent (still in the womb) all the way to new first-round draft pick. Like all first-round draft picks, there will be an unveiling and tons of excitement. The birth will bring together family and friends just like a draft party.

You also have to decide whether to go by "Dad," "Daddy," or "Father." "Father" sounds stuffy and formal but works for some families. "Daddy" is what my star calls me. Many daughters will continue to use "Daddy" as you age, especially when they are asking for money. Most sons will shift from

SPREADING THE WORD THE FASTEST WAY

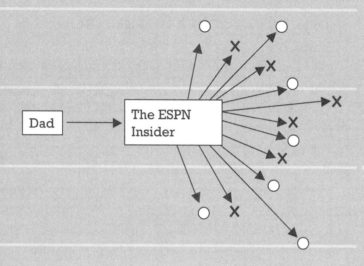

The memories created with your little prospect will delight you for years to come.

Your first emotion is going to be a gut feeling; it is okay to be scared.

Many people wait twelve weeks to tell people.

Many grandmothers get more excited than mothers.

You might choose to tell the ESPN insider to spread the word.

You will have to become used to getting congratulated for being pregnant.

You usually can't find out the sex of the child until sixteen to twenty weeks into the pregnancy.

Balance being a guy and a man when you become a dad.

You just signed a twenty-year (or longer) contract.

"Daddy" to "Dad" as they grow older—unless they call you from the principal's office.

WORKING TOGETHER ON THE FIELD

Earlier I referred to my wife as my teammate. In a perfect world, all decisions would be mutually agreed upon and easy choices to make. In reality it is usually more complicated than that. Moms and dads will probably slip into roles when it comes to having and caring for your newborn. It will be beneficial to attempt to understand these now.

For thousands of years, guys were the hunters and providers and women did all of the home stuff. Thankfully, those roles have blended over the last thirty years or so. With the increased role of women in the workplace, dads must take on a more active role on the home front. But keep in mind that we are still fighting thousands of years of history in figuring out our roles.

Most women have a mommy gene that just comes with all the other female equipment. They react quicker to the baby and can even sense danger before it happens. Most guys are great dads, but we don't have baby ESP. The mommy gene is the result of thousands of years of history and is more prevalent in humans than any other species. Most animals give birth to multiple young, hoping a few survive. Humans usually give birth to one at a time, and we expect it to survive. Since guys don't have baby ESP, luckily we have ESPN.

The roles in the house may change over time, so remember to be flexible. Caring for the baby will be a shared responsibility that may ebb and flow between the partners in today's world. But most pre-baby decisions will still be made by the mom.

The QB

In most homes, the dad will be the quarterback (QB). Even if you never took a center snap in your life, you are now the QB of your team when it comes to having and caring for your baby. The QB is responsible for keeping the team morale up and leadership and is crucial for on-the-field decisions. He also gives his opinion in the meeting rooms and thoroughly scouts the opposition. QB roles have evolved in the last thirty years from player to player-coach. We are much more responsible when it comes to childhood decisions than dads were thirty years ago. Chances are your dad never had the input in baby matters that you will.

QB dad is a new breed of more involved dads. And it sounds better than soccer mom. And don't even mention the phrase *soccer dad*.

 QB dad: *You, the on-field leader of your team.*

As the QB dad, you will eventually realize that your newly won trophy cries, spits up, poops, and is the cutest person in the world. You keep the title of QB dad as your child grows up. You also get to keep the leadership and admiration that comes with having the baby.

The most important advice I can give new dads is this: You only get one chance to raise your kids. Regardless of how it may seem, new coaching jobs or business promotions will always be there if you are talented. You can climb Mount Everest when you are forty-five and run a triathlon at sixty, but your kids will only be young once. Enjoy that time and embrace it.

It may be a cliché, but nobody on their deathbed ever wished that they spent more time at work. Talk to and listen to your kids from day one to establish a bond. Building a relationship with your kids before they become teenagers is vital. And let's face it; most kids need guidance during their teen years. If the head coach and QB dad can't give advice, they will seek other's advice.

Enjoy your new role as QB dad. You get to be team leader, and many eyes will be focused on you in the coming months (unless the head coach is with you). If she is with you, just step back and let her bask in the moment. Your moments are coming in the next year. All of your photo opportunities will come after the baby arrives. And let's face it; for the first twenty-four hours the baby will be just like a newly won Super Bowl trophy—admired, held up, photographed, and passed among all interested parties.

The Head Coach

If you are the QB dad, then mom becomes the head coach in baby decisions. She makes all of the big decisions about having your baby. As the QB dad, feel free to give input and be supportive, but be prepared to be overruled on many baby decisions. After all, she is the one who is going to attempt to push a football through a garden hose. One of the first decisions your partner will make as head coach is where to have the baby. The head coach will make the decision on where to have the baby.

Most guys think hospitals are the only place to have a baby. We are a simple breed that imagines all babies come into the world surrounded by people in scrubs. The head coach will research where to have the baby and find out that you have many choices. She may even ask for your opinion in this choice. Of course, it's more likely she will just tell you where to show up.

The head coach will also make a decision about what methods of pain treatment she wants. If guys could give birth, we would go for epidurals, morphine, codeine, Demerol, and anything else needed to numb the pain. We might even ask for all of them together after watching the birth video. Most guys have a high tolerance of pain, after the fact. If you break a bone in a football game, you gut it out. But if we know pain is coming, we react differently. We don't volunteer to have cavities filled without drugs, but many women will elect to have a baby without drugs. This is her choice alone. Give input and be supportive, but keep in mind you don't get a vote on this one.

Breast-feeding will also be a solo choice. She will value your opinion, and then she will tell you if she has decided to go with formula or breast. One area where your vote might actually count is when you're deciding whether to go for cloth or disposable diapers. Since you are going to change some diapers, she will want your input. Be aware that you can't arm-wrestle to break ties. Just think football and fire hose.

Like you, the head coach just wants to raise a healthy, happy child. She is just as concerned about the baby's well-being as you are. Before your star enters the field of play and for most of the first year, she will make most of the baby decisions. After that, you may do a better job of working as a team in making shared choices.

The Owner

You are the QB dad and your partner is the head coach. Soon after arriving at your home stadium (your house), you are going to realize there is another part to any good team. All good teams need an owner. The team owner will be the baby! Just like on most NFL teams, when the owner speaks, the QB dad and the head coach spring into action. The QB dad and the head coach are going to act on the whim of the owner. For at least the first year, the baby will rule almost all decisions.

 The cherished moments shared with the owner will make it easier to deal with the lost sleep.

Fumble

The owner will wake you up in the middle of the night and pull you toward the changing table at inopportune moments. The owner will also keep you home at night and drain your bank account. But the owner will make you smile, laugh, and bring many happy moments for both the QB dad and the head coach. Lost sleep is a given with raising a newborn, but it will be balanced by all of those precious smiles.

Help on the Sidelines

Think of all the wonderful people that are willing to pitch in and help as assistant coaches. From parents, in-laws, friends, and coworkers, you will find out most people love babies. And they love helping new parents. This aid can come in all forms, from food to free baby-sitting. Enjoy this help and encourage it. You get much-needed help and they feel better that they could pitch in. All parts of the team need to work together to win the big game.

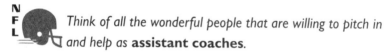

Think of all the wonderful people that are willing to pitch in and help as **assistant coaches**.

In the next year you are going to get more advice than you want. Ignore most of that advice (unless, of course, it comes from this book). Think of all the people giving that advice as armchair quarterbacks. Unless they are willing to roll up their sleeves and get to work, ignore them. You will even get armchair-quarterback advice from people without kids. Everybody is going to raise perfect kids before they have them.

A ton of free advice will come from **armchair quarterbacks**.

You are also going to have to deal with Monday morning quarterbacks. They are people who are going to give you advice after the fact. After you tell a fatherhood or pregnancy story, they are going to jump in and tell you what you should have done. Gee, thanks. Listen, be polite, and try to remember to never tell them another story. It is very easy to be a Monday morning quarterback.

As your team expands, your roles will become more defined. The roles may slightly change as your star enters the world. The roles may even change from day to day. Raising a newborn takes patience and a sense of humor. That is amazing. Those same qualities are also needed in dealing with a pregnant head coach.

Touchdown

Dealing with a newborn takes flexibility, a sense of humor, and a good dose of patience.

Embrace the fact that you are going to be a QB dad. Throwing the ball with your little superstar in the future will make all of the sleepless nights worth it. And as any good QB knows, the head coach and the QB form a partnership on any successful team.

THE NEW TEAM

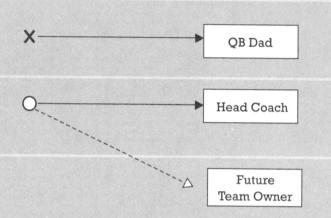

X ————————▶ QB Dad

O ————————▶ Head Coach

△ Future Team Owner

Raising great kids is a goal of all new dads.

The dad will act like the quarterback of the team.

The new mom becomes the head coach in baby decisions.

Be prepared to be overruled on many baby decisions.

You only get one chance to raise your kids.

Build trust with your kids before they become teenagers.

The QB dad and the head coach are going to act on the whim of the owner.

Parents, in-laws, friends, and coworkers can all be thought of as assistant coaches.

Patience and the ability to laugh will be vital in the coming years.

2. TRAINING CAMP

Training camp is in full swing now as you prepare for the arrival of your own little tailback. All of your friends know by this juncture. Be kind, thoughtful, take an active role, and ensure a smooth transition as your family grows.

Your partner will probably begin to show during the beginning of the second trimester. Acquaintances may wonder if she is pregnant or has just decided to eat her way through all of Baskin-Robbins' thirty-one flavors. Asking my wife was unnecessary since she was beaming out 100,000-watt smiles. Of course, if you told the ESPN insider, many will already know.

The size of your partner's bump won't be the only thing that changes during the second trimester. From your future star becoming a kicker that rivals Adam Vinatieri to your teammate becoming a nympho, you should be prepared for everything you thought you knew to change.

VISITING FANS

Be prepared for complete strangers to want to rub your teammate's belly as they figure it out. This will get worse as you head toward D day. Strangers will see her in the grocery store and they will want to rub the Buddha belly that contains your child. They won't ask, but your teammate can probably stop them by shrieking in terror as they approach her. You can also determine a polite way to ask them not to. I still like the shrieking in terror idea, but my wife refused.

 Fumble *Strangers will want to rub your partner's belly after she starts to show. Does it bring them good luck?*

If they are over seventy, I'm afraid even shrieking won't stop them. I think babies make the elderly feel young. Old people adore babies, and your little tailback is going to get hundreds of smiles and waves from the elderly.

Some old people will also often just randomly give your future all-star money. In the grocery store line, gray-haired people will share the wealth. Your star just has to learn to reach out to grab the cash. Be sure to teach her this skill early. Your baby doesn't understand money yet, so pocket it and enjoy.

FIRST RUNNING PLAYS

The second trimester of pregnancy is when the baby actually starts to move around. The first movement of the fetus will feel like butterflies or guppies in your teammate's tummy. When she feels this, rejoice with her. Don't dare mention that it might be gas from that Indian food you had for dinner. Put your hand on her belly and share the moment. You won't feel anything, but she does. Imagine your little tailback just caught her first pitch and is turning the corner.

 Fumble *When the head coach feels butterflies, don't dare suggest it might be gas.*

Kicks will be the first thing you feel through the head coach's tummy. My little one would practice her punting every night as we sat and relaxed. She will be an all-pro kicker someday. As we wound down for the day, she would wind up. All day long, the head coach moving around rocked her to sleep. At night she was ready to go. When the head coach lay down to sleep, the exercises would begin.

Many doctors theorize that is why many babies have backwards sleep patterns when they enter the outside world. In the first few months, babies will want to party all night and sleep during the day. For several months, I was convinced we had given birth to a rock star, or a college freshman.

Later in the pregnancy you may actually see your partner's stomach become square as the little one flexes and kicks. Some people say that the baby is trying to get out. But why would the baby want out? Life in the womb must be pretty good. Let's see, mom is doing the breathing, mom is doing the eating, mom is keeping her boss happy, and the QB dad is worrying if he'll be a good enough dad. Somebody eats for you, breathes for you, and no annoying bills arrive in the mail. Except for the eating part (I like to eat!), that sounds like a pretty sweet deal. Of course, she has been swimming in her own pee, kind of like a ten-year-old boy in the pool at summer camp. Though, most of us liked summer camp.

No wonder they cry when they see the doctor for the first time. I wondered if my star was crying because she saw me, but she was more likely crying because it was time to go to work.

QB-HEAD COACH PRIVATE MEETINGS

Prepare yourself for the *best* part of training camp. Most women in the second trimester may also begin to show you a side that may be different than normal. I'm talking about pure lust. For many couples, no-holds-barred sex is frequent during this time. There are several theories on why this happens—from not having to worry about getting pregnant (duh!) to increased blood supply. The heck with science, if it happens to you, enjoy.

Touchdown

Most women will exhibit pure lust during the second trimester. If it happens to you, congrats.

If your partner shows no signs of becoming a sex kitten, leave this book open to this section in a place where she is bound to see it. Natural curiosity to see what you are reading will compel her to read it. Most women hate being different. Try not to let her see this paragraph or she may be wise to your trick.

The coffee table will eventually be off limits for sex, so take advantage of this time to have fun. At this time, all positions are probably still allowed. The ob/gyn can establish rules and guidelines for sex. The ob/gyn will be the referee for dos and don'ts. But normally there aren't many don'ts. You also don't have to worry about a little one walking in on you. Create a few memories in other rooms of your castle. You can't do this when she is twelve unless you want to scar her for life. Many of us overheard or saw something we wished we hadn't in our formative years.

Pure unbridled passion is a great thing. My motto is get while the getting is good, but respect her wishes. She might even be up for two-a-days, if you know what I mean. I didn't know how good I had it and also didn't know what was coming after the baby entered the real world. Your passionate partner may slow down after the little one is breathing for herself. Take advantage of every opportunity you are provided now. If she gives you the green light, go for it.

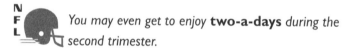 *You may even get to enjoy* **two-a-days** *during the second trimester.*

When she gives you the stop sign, don't try and talk her out of it. Her body is going through a myriad of hormonal changes and she deserves the right to be finicky. Very late in the pregnancy, your teammate might be too tired. Realize, as our ob/gyn put it, "she has a parasite growing inside her."

It seems silly to say this, but you also can't do any damage to the fetus by having sex. Many men are worried (as I was) that they might hurt their little quarterback. It just isn't true. Orgasms (hers, not yours) are actually very enjoyable for the mother.

PASSING

Another benefit of your partner being pregnant will only be understood by guys. Let's face it; guys and women are different. Actually guys and men are different. This is shown in no place better than the gas department. And I am not talking about unleaded. Yep, we're talking butt gas. Guys not only enjoy farting, but they revel in it (and most guys love to share the wealth). Most women (and even some men) don't. It is one of those great things that make us different. I, for one, am glad that men and women are different.

You will also be challenged for your throne as the king of the gas pump. The head coach will become better at passing gas than your best friend in high school. My head coach became world class for a few months. She would lie in bed and make my eyes water. It made me proud. Reluctantly, you may have to pass the crown for a few months. I have confidence you can win back the crown, but not until the kid is breathing for herself.

Training camp is a place where guys can be guys. Passing gas will become a sport. In many ways, the head coach will get temporary guy status.

THE PRESEASON NAME

You and the head coach need a way to talk about your little star. "Baby," "kid," "youngster," and "parasite" could all be acceptable (well, maybe calling her "parasite" is not a great idea). Better yet, come up with some creative name or steal one—Chip for chip off the old block, Tiger, Spike, Big Ben. I stole a name from my friend April—Cletus the Fetus. I spent six months calling our child Cletus while she was *in utero*. When we found out it was a she, I still stuck with Cletus. My wife ruled out calling her Cletus after she was born (darn!). So pick a name to call the officially unnamed fetus until you decide on an official name. My wife insisted that I couldn't say fetus until twelve weeks, so we called her Elmo the Embryo up until then.

Touchdown

If you haven't decided on a name for the kid, you need some way to communicate about your little prospect.

If you don't come up with a name, you could always use "it." That seems like a pretty lame way to talk about your future star. "Baby," "fetus," and "embryo" would work, but they sound like you are talking about someone else's child. Personalize the preseason name, but don't get too attached to it. If my head coach and I ever have a boy, I am fighting hard for Cletus as a permanent name.

LINEBACKER OR CHEERLEADER

As a team, you and your partner are going to have to make the decision about finding out the sex of the child. Around the twenty-week mark, experts can begin to make educated guesses from the ultrasound. You will be looking over their shoulder and might be able to make out the head, but that will be about it. Guys will misread the ultrasound when looking at it; all guys will assume they are having a son (must be something about that umbilical cord that mixes us up). The experts are occasionally wrong, but advances in ultrasound technology make mistakes less common.

Fumble *Many men looking at ultrasounds are convinced they are having boys until the nurse points out that they were looking at the umbilical cord.*

You must make everybody aware if you don't want to know the gender. Wear a giant "Hello my name is 'We don't want to know the sex of our child'" sticker on any trips to the ultrasound place or doctor's office. My wife's best friend Kim was accidentally told by an unsuspecting nurse. The nurse said "she sure looks healthy" and the cat was out of the bag. She saw Kim's mouth drop open in shock and tried to cover by saying she called all babies she, but it was too late. Finding out the sex of the child is a purely personal choice. You will hear plenty of advice on this topic.

If you are unsure about wanting to find out the sex, the doctor can write the sex and put it in a sealed envelope. This will allow you and your teammate to find out at a time of your choice. You can plan a nice romantic dinner with just the two of you. You could also invite the family and friends over and have an unveiling party.

If you really have your heart set on a boy, try to talk your partner into finding out the sex ahead of time. This will give you several weeks to deal with any feelings. You are going to be in a position in the delivery room to see the baby before your partner. Your eyes will give you away if you are set on having a boy. Your teammate will probably be looking at your face as the baby leaves her body. Trust me, you are going to love whatever you have, but some men are just set on having boys first.

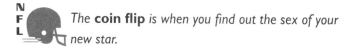 *The **coin flip** is when you find out the sex of your new star.*

In a completely unscientific poll of the people I know, a throwback trend appeared. The surprise factor is making a comeback. Many QB dads and head coaches want the excitement of finding out in the delivery room and the joy of going out into the waiting room to tell family and friends. You could actually keep this joy, if you are very good at keeping secrets. My head coach had a friend who elected not to find out, but her family and boss knew the sex of her baby. She swears that she did not know until the hospital.

Chromosomal analysis (CA) is a sure-fire way to know the sex of your little star. CA is a long way of saying "boy or girl for sure." Be aware that ultrasounds can be misread, leading you to pick the wrong sex name (although false readings are fairly rare nowadays).

We elected to find out the sex, although we were more concerned with the health of the baby than the sex of Cletus. We also had an amniocentesis because my wife was over thirty-five. The amnio test left absolutely no doubt. I was having a girl! A fellow football coach, Bill Van Cleve (whose first child was a girl), told me that she would reach into my heart and wrap it around her finger the first time I saw her. Bill is a wise man. "Daddy's girl" is a common phrase for a reason.

THE MOST BEAUTIFUL WOMAN IN THE WORLD

Your partner may be as big as a pulling guard by now, but she will probably be glowing. This is the woman you adore and she is having your baby. The feelings you already have for her will intensify. She will look fabulous as she rounds into shape to deliver your star. Most men (and women) think a pregnant feminine shape is one of the most beautiful sights to behold. Long before super skinny models were in vogue, people worshipped voluptuous women.

Starting at about five months into the pregnancy, another wonderful thing happens—the booby fairy shows up. If your head coach is on the small side, she will become voluptuous. If she is already voluptuous, watch out. Of course, the booby fairy is a practical joker since her breasts are being primed for a different purpose. And they will become too tender to handle late in pregnancy.

Yes, your head coach will be nervous about many of the same concerns that worry you. She will also be feeling tremendous excitement as the day approaches. This excitement will show in her eyes and face. She has probably focused on eating better during the last few months. She is eating plenty of veggies and religiously taking her multivitamin. This will show up in her overall appearance. Her face and skin will look radiant. In addition to better nutrition, nature also goes into overdrive to help her produce a healthy baby. Hair and nails will appear to go on a growing spurt.

Her hair will look luxurious at this time. My head coach always talked about her nails looking so great. To most guys, nails are like pro offensive linemen. You only notice them when something is wrong. Tackles, guards, and centers only get mentioned when they jump offsides or hold a defensive lineman. Women's nails only get noticed when they are dirty or have been recently chewed. Most women do their nails for other women, not guys.

Pregnant women also raid their QB dad's closet. Most guys like the look of a woman wearing an oversized guy's dress shirt or our old college sweatshirt. Pregnant women actually adopt pieces of our clothing for the last few months of pregnancy, but most guys like it. We enjoy eating Saturday morning breakfast while she is wearing one of our dress shirts. So watching her wear one at night while we talk is a turn on. She may be wearing it because it is the only thing that fits, but we still like it.

Touchdown

 My head coach looked absolutely fabulous as we approached draft day. She was also the perfect size for running interference in a grocery store.

Training camp is in full swing now. The baby might be dreading leaving the womb, but the QB dad and the head coach are both excited. Of course, there will be bumps along the way, but training camp has wonderful benefits so enjoy.

THE WORST PART OF TRAINING CAMP

Like all training camps, preparing for the new youngster has its share of incomplete passes. While the possible ferocity of your teammate's libido may be very welcome, some parts of camp just aren't any fun. Food cravings, food aversions, morning sickness, and fluctuating moods will all be incomplete passes. Baby classes aren't much fun, but they are a necessary evil. You take the good with the bad, and many years from now you and your partner will laugh at some of the things that happen in the buildup to draft day.

TOUCHDOWNS AND INTERCEPTIONS

Most moms develop some weird type of food craving or an intense dislike or aversion. I was fortunate on both accounts; my wife had zero cravings or aversions while she was pregnant. Her mood changes and morning sickness were also very minor; I thanked her every day for those small miracles. I coach defense now and those miracles were as comforting as an eight-minute drive when our team was ahead.

 If your teammate is pregnant in Green Bay in the middle of
Fumble *winter, two words of advice: snow chains.*

Food cravings are actually kind of funny. You and your teammate will laugh about her cravings for years to come. Pickles and ice cream is the first craving most people think of, but cravings run the gamut from jalapenos to fried chicken. A food craving is like a touchdown, guaranteed to bring the head coach joy. When cravings strike, it is probably better to be living near a major town. Twenty-four-hour drive-throughs and all night grocery stores will become your friend.

THE BEST PART OF TRAINING CAMP

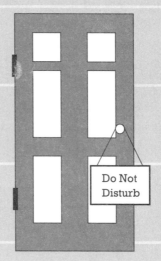

Do Not Disturb

Complete strangers want to rub the head coach's belly after she begins to show.

As a group, old people love babies.

The second trimester of pregnancy is when the baby actually starts to move around.

Most women become very passionate during the second trimester.

Sex is usually okay, but check with her doctor.

You need a pet name to use when talking about your little star.

Let everybody know if you don't want to know the gender before birth.

Let me back up for a minute. I said that my wife had no cravings because of her pregnancy. Well, she always craves chocolate and probably always will. While we were pregnant, the results of a Finnish study were released in *USA Today* that said women who ate chocolate every day during the pregnancy were going to give birth to happy babies that will cry less. My wife definitely has a fondness for the Finns now. We loaded the house up with all manners of candy for this time. It worked; we have a healthy and sweet-natured baby.

Once the head coach has established her cravings, stock up the fridge and freezer. Hopefully whatever she craves can be frozen, because these cravings can change. The cravings can change from day to day. Hell, they can change from minute to minute. The two-minute drill might be you running to the store every night.

 The **two-minute drill** *will consist of you running to the store to satisfy your teammates's craving.*

A food aversion is when a particular food sends your head coach into spasms as she runs for the door. Food aversions are the interceptions of the food game, guaranteed to make the head coach bury her head in shame. My wife's best friend, Kim, was repulsed by the smell of orange juice. The mere smell or mention of OJ sent her into kvetching fits. She literally sounded like a cat coughing up a fur ball. Kim's aversions eventually grew to include tomato sauce after a dinner of my world-famous meatball sandwiches.

Many women have also repeated to me an intense dislike for all manner of foods or smells. My wife is Italian (and a fabulous cook), and if she had suffered from an aversion for tomato sauce I might have had to move out. No pizza or pasta? It would have been bad. Food aversions should be easy to deal with unless they involve your favorite food. If they do, you have to realize the head coach's happiness rules the house.

 If a food aversion involves your favorite food, you have to **Fumble** *take one for the team and abstain for a period of time.*

You might also want to fill the glove compartment of your car, or anyplace you will spend a significant amount of time, with small snacks. The urge to eat will strike at a moment's notice and can disappear just as fast. Sometimes only a single bite is needed to satisfy this need. Keep trail mix or some other easy-to-grab snack handy for when these moments arise. Often my head coach would be hit with an instant need or desire for food, so we stocked the car. She was happy. And, as you'll learn, if your teammate is happy, everybody is happy.

MORNING SICKNESS

Morning sickness is an unpleasant side effect of pregnancy. My teammate and I were fortunate, but many aren't so lucky. It strikes many women during pregnancy. Consider yourself lucky if it avoids your house. Morning sickness is actually the way many women find out they are pregnant. It starts around the fifth week, so it would correspond with having a late period. The good news is that it generally disappears around sixteen weeks and won't cause any damage to the baby. The exact cause is a mystery to the experts, but it is a real concern.

For morning sickness, you have to be understanding (and **Fumble** *carry a bucket for her to ralph into).*

From my observations, the bouts are often short in duration, so just be supportive. They are also not just confined to the morning. The bouts will consist of nausea and vomiting at all levels. She may just have to sit down and rest for the bout to pass; she may also sprint to the porcelain throne. A heightened sense of smell is another side effect; she may grow to hate your sneakers for the next few months. If the bouts are particularly bad on a regular basis, talk to your ob/gyn for advice. As long as she stays hydrated and keeps some food down, no permanent damage will occur. You wouldn't let anybody play quarterback that sick, so heed the advice of the specialists. If your teammate decides to go to the doctor to talk about her morning sickness, go with her! In fact, as I've said before, go to every possible ob appointment with your partner. Don't be afraid to ask questions. The doctors and nurses in ob clinics love kids and moms; it is why they do what they do. They will be glad to help.

Eating small amounts of food and drinking all the time will help morning sickness. Of course, you will gain weight and may be hung over (sorry, it's the head coach who needs the help). And encourage her to stay away from alcohol. There are also many other anecdotal treatments such as ginger, dry toast, aromatherapy, and my wife's own favorite, chocolate. My wife even faked symptoms to eat chocolate. There is no proof that chocolate works, but it kept my head coach happy.

MOOD SWINGS

As your future star grows inside your teammate, her chemistry is continually changing, which will cause her to act irrational at times. Hormone changes are one of the major side effects of pregnancy. What was perfectly okay five minutes ago will now send her into a raving fit. Remember that this is not a reflection on you. After a few minutes or a good nap she will be back to normal. It's not her fault; blame it on chemistry.

Fumble

Mood swings are not her fault; blame it on chemistry.

Hormonal changes will cause her to be irritable one minute and sweet the next. Take the good with the bad and remember these words: *Yes, Dear.* You can lessen the mood swings by killing them with kindness. Treat mood swings like commercials: a necessary evil that is over in two minutes. But no remote will enable you to change this channel. And by all means, if she has a craving, execute the two-minute drill to perfection and make her happy. When Momma's happy, everybody's happy.

Mood swings appear to be the worst during the first and last trimesters. In the first trimester, she is going through tons of physical changes as the "parasite" grows inside her.

She will be dealing with stress, fatigue, metabolism changes, and varying hormone levels.

Not only are there physical changes for her, but there are emotional changes as well. She will have to deal with tons of fears. Will she be a good enough mom? Will birth be painful? Will the QB dad still find her sexy? How can we afford this? Will she do a better job than her parents?

Touchdown

The baby blues and postpartum depression are serious and should be treated as such.

As the QB dad, you get to avoid the physical changes but not the emotional ones. As it settles in, you are going to wonder about many of the same issues. You might put on a few sympathetic "pregnancy" pounds. You will be wrestling with the same emotional issues as her. The key to dealing with emotional issues is talking. Many guys would rather have dental fillings than talk. Pregnancy is one time it is okay to talk a lot.

Try to spend a little time every day listening to her. Guys like to fix problems. Most of her pregnancy-related emotional problems can't be fixed. Just let her vent (and occasionally rant and rave). Ask her questions about how she is feeling. Try to wait thirty seconds after she says anything before you answer. She might not want answers, just support. It also helps to relay some of your fears to her.

As she grows, there are a few things that you don't want to say. Never, under any circumstances, call her Big Momma or the Big Lady. You pretty much want to avoid the word *big* in any conversation. As a matter of fact, eliminate *big, large, gigantic, humongous, rotund,* and *voluptuous* from your vocabulary for the next year. If she hears any one of these words she could potentially break into tears. And it will be your fault.

If a down mood swing lasts more than a few days, suggest she mention it to her doctor. Then duck, in case she throws a shoe at you.

Depression is fairly common and can be treated. After the baby is born, you also need to be on the lookout for a more serious form of depression. Postpartum depression is a very serious medical condition that you will need to keep an eye out for. It will be discussed in more detail in Chapter 13.

BABY CLASSES

Your dad probably didn't have to go to class to have a baby, but you won't be so lucky. You are most likely going to have to attend at least one type of class. These classes are one of the final requirements to get you into the new dad fraternity: I Smell Poo.

Birth education classes come in all shapes and sizes. The head coach will pick out one type and you will just go. My advice here? Deal with it. Not many guys want to go, but since the 1980s we just do. If you try to get out of this, you will be viewed as unkind and uncaring. In extremely rare cases, the head coach will choose someone else to be her birth coach and you might be out of this duty.

The choices for this type of class run from a one-day basic birth education class to weekly evening classes that last for months. Be aware: These classes are run by women for women. Once again, you will feel like a bit player in this pregnancy, as will all the other happy dads at the classes. You may even have to attend two different types of classes. The good news is you probably only have to go for your first-round draft pick. If you have later draft picks, you will be baby educated.

There are several bonuses to going to these classes. One, going willingly will make the head coach happy. Two, you will meet other QB dads going through the same things and may develop lasting friendships. Friendships with other couples with kids are a good thing. Three, you might actually learn something. And finally, you get to see a free slasher film. Actually, it's a birth film. You can now think of the doctor as Jason and Michael Myers wrapped into one. Try not to call the doc Hannibal at your next appointment. If you are really squeamish, head for the bathroom during the movie.

Types of Classes

The standard one-day class will almost always be on a Saturday and will take the bulk of the day. You might get home for the late afternoon college games, but you will miss the noon games if it is in the fall. But it will be over in just one Saturday. The weekly classes will last six to eight weeks. They are almost always on Tuesdays, and that is a good thing. I read somewhere years ago that Tuesday is the least likely night for sex among married couples. Also, unless it is a major bowl game, no reputable football games are played on Tuesday.

The one-day variety will cover all of the basics and provides a good overview. It will go through all of the pain management choices (for the head coach, not you), vaginal births versus C-sections, and postbirth stuff. You may also get other good hints. They are usually sponsored by the hospital/birth center. They may even be required by the hospital, and they may feed you lunch.

Fumble

Laughing during a baby class is never a good idea.

The once-a-week classes are usually geared toward some method of birth. The Lamaze and Bradley methods are the two most common. Both of these choices involve teaching you how to breathe. Amazing, you have been breathing since birth, but now you need a class to teach you again. (Question—if you fail breathing class, would you still have the baby?) Go to the class, be supportive, and have a good time. Both of you will laugh about these classes later. Memo to all QB dads—don't laugh during the class.

Learning about Pain Methods

The head coach will learn how to cope with pain using alternative methods. Most women still opt for traditional methods of pain relief (drugs), but there are other choices. My favorite is vocal toning (wailing a single vowel sound at the top of your lungs for several minutes). Pro athletes usually use drugs when they go under the knife, but some women refuse drugs when they have a baby. I can almost see my favorite NFL linebacker wailing his way through knee surgery. My personal favorite method of giving birth has to be hypnobirthing. Being in a trance and enjoying the pain of childbirth is definitely a foreign concept to guys. I don't enjoy pain now and probably won't enjoy it tomorrow.

There are so many choices out there, and you will be instructed by the head coach which one you will attend. Keep your head up, go, and try to have a good time. It will all be worth it the first time you see your number one draft pick.

Training camp has good and bad sides. Many of the bad sides will bring you chuckles for many years. Enjoy the laughs later; you probably won't laugh when you are living them. Morning sickness bouts, mood swings, and baby classes are not laughing matters at the time. The memories will fade as you approach draft day. Shortly you will have a new star to spoil.

THE WORST PART OF TRAINING CAMP

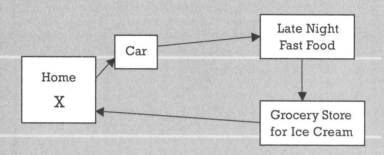

Midnight Two-Minute Drill

Strange food cravings are natural.

Food aversions are also going to happen.

Morning sickness isn't restricted to the morning.

Stock the car and the house with snacks.

Go to as many doctor appointments as possible.

Listen to her as she talks; she may have both fear and apprehension.

Mood swings are natural; fight back with kindness.

Remember these months; you will laugh about them for years.

SELECTING THE EQUIPMENT AND
3. LOCKER ROOM

Just like football players have certain needs, so does your baby. Cups, helmets, and girdles aren't fun to wear but are required nonetheless. You will have to outfit your locker room with all of the baby needs. Much of the needed baby stuff will be bought by others. All you have to do is prepare a list of goodies that you and your partner decide the little star will need. This means an entire day (and possibly weekend) of shopping.

Touchdown

The best part about outfitting a baby is that other people will buy you most of the stuff, at least for the first little linebacker.

It is a common myth that guys don't like shopping. Guys have perpetuated this myth over many generations. Keep the myth alive! Guys like to shop, we just do it differently. We shop with a purpose; well, actually two. One, to actually bring something we want home. The key word here is *want*; we don't like shopping for needs. We want remote control cars, retro football jerseys, ATVs, audio equipment, books,

DVDs, and sporting goods. There is absolutely no problem shopping for these items. Guys just aren't fans of shopping for window blinds and toilet paper. You will have to shop for needs eventually, but that can wait until the baby gets closer to leaving the womb. The second purpose is to minimize the time in stores that don't sell remote control cars, retro football jerseys, ATVs, books, DVDs, audio equipment, and sporting goods. In those stores, our goal is to get in and out as fast as possible without creating a rift with our partner.

EQUIPPING YOUR STAR

One Saturday will need to be reserved for registering for baby stuff. Schedule around football games, but don't let your head coach know. Suggest heading off to the store at 8 AM to beat the rush. You might be home in time for the late afternoon games. Keep your sense of humor as you head to the Big Box Baby Superstore. You will also need the patience of a kindergarten teacher. There is virtually no way to minimize the time while registering for baby stuff. Do *not* suggest that she register with the help of her mom, sister, or gal pals. This is a task that you have to endure. Suck it up and deal with it. You are going to be a good dad and husband; registering is just a required task. Do not try to plan any other activity for registration day. It is a day for you and your partner.

In the NFL they now have training sessions called OTAs (optional team activities). These off-season practices may not be required, but just miss a few and see what happens. Registering for baby stuff can be considered an OTA. Don't miss it.

You can save some time by researching car seats, high chairs, and cribs before you go. Find Web sites that will compare all of the different types and give you pros and cons of each. You find the sites, then let your teammate read them and decide together. Safety is the number one concern for all of the big items. Money is not an issue when it comes to safety.

OTAs are optional team activities that aren't really optional. Registering for baby stuff is an OTA.

Saturday morning arrives and you load up to head to the store. As you enter Big Box Baby Superstore, you are amazed that a store this large doesn't contain remote control cars, retro football jerseys, ATVs, books, DVDs, audio equipment, and sporting goods. Well, there are a few books. You are greeted by a cheerful helper just inside the door. She sits down with you and gets real personal. After a few moments with her, you realize that she could steal your identity; she knows everything about you and your partner. After taking your data, a bank of computers light up behind her and the printer starts printing. The printer spits out a ream of paper . . . actually only eight to twelve pages. You can just check off what you need. Some stores give you a barcode scanner to speed up the process. This is a gun that looks like something out of *Star Wars*. This ray gun, however, is actually a handheld scanner that zaps UPC codes for all the stuff you really need (and maybe some stuff you don't need). The scanner is fun to play with. You just zap stuff and it will appear on your registry. Zap as much fun stuff as you can, like giant jars of animal crackers, individual jars of baby food, packs of base-ball cards, single sodas, and packs of gum. You can zap things when your partner isn't looking. How did they have babies in the early days?

Fumble *I feel confident my grandmothers didn't need this much baby stuff and my parents are almost completely normal.*

Armed with clipboard, two pencils, and the barcode scanner, you head off into the depths of the store. Staring at twenty-four feet of different types of baby bottles, you never had any idea that there are so many kinds of baby bottles. You not only have to decide size, but you also have to choose nipple type. This is a required day that every guy has gone through in the last twenty-five years. Your dad probably never helped your mother register, but that was the old days.

Looking at the list, you might see a few things to take exception to, like a heated baby wipe warmer! "I don't get heated toilet paper"; you might logically say. Does a baby really need heated wipes? I feel confident that this is an extravagance that is only lavished on people with tons of friends.

Mandatory Equipment

In my opinion there are several must-haves. Strollers are similar to a sideline during a football game. They are where your number one draft pick is going to spend a great deal of time early in her career. One of the most useful purchases that can be made is the travel system. The travel system integrates a carrier, car seat, and a stroller into one package. Since newborns sleep somewhere between fourteen and eighteen hours a day, having a carrier to move her about in is wonderful. The carrier fits into the stroller and car seat with no need to wake your little star. The carrier also gives you a chance to get in a set of bicep curls, since time in the gym could be limited.

Another great item is a diaper pail that comes with film to hermetically seal diapers. Diaper pails are an engineering marvel. They have a canister full of plastic film that feeds down into the bottom of the pail. You push the diaper down and it gets encased in the plastic, and when you twist the top it seals the diaper into a caca cocoon. When you empty it, you cut the film and tie it off. When you open the bottom, you will pull out a string of diapers that looks like a giant set of pearls. The QB dad will be responsible for emptying it. When you empty the diaper pail, you can make the largest necklaces ever. Baby poop does not have an odor initially, but once the baby starts solid foods, watch out. The film is scented to mask the odor and does a decent job of hiding the smell. Competition is good: I once stuffed forty-three diapers into the pail before emptying it. The necklace was twenty-two feet long. Try to beat my record.

You will also want onesies, and lots of them. Onesies are one-piece (duh!) outfits that snap under the crotch for easy access at changing time. Added benefit—they are available with any college or pro team's logo on them. Make sure that you get onesies with snaps only. As a matter of fact, all children's clothing should only come with snaps until size 3T. By then you can start teaching the kid to use buttons.

Another must-have is a bouncer seat. These are soft, padded seats that are like little slings for the baby. They have a bar of colorful toys and things that are at eye height for the baby. Most have an electric vibrating motor that rocks the baby gently to sleep. They are like a baby-sized version of the massaging loungers sold in high-priced gadget stores. The bouncer is easy to move from room to room and is a great place for your little tailback to nap.

Be prepared to spend a minimum of thirty minutes in each of the baby aisles. Luckily, some aisles can be avoided since they are for older kids. Your partner will probably have much more patience when debating the merits of high-flow and low-flow nipples. Give your opinion and try to act interested. Just face up to the fact that it is going to take a whole day at Big Box Baby Superstore. People are going to buy you stuff for the baby, that is just a fact. You want the stuff they buy to be useful.

 When asked for your input on baby gear, never say "I don't care," even if you don't care.

Fumble

Your partner will also want to register at Big Box Everything Superstore; go along with it. Two stores is a must in today's full-throttle world. Insist that you visit both on the same day, if possible. You will be very supportive, and the second store won't take as long. Besides, this store may actually have remote control cars, retro football jerseys, ATVs, books, DVDs, audio equipment, and sporting goods. You might be able to sneak a few of these items onto your registry list if your teammate is not looking. A helpful hint—get her a large bottled water after you leave the baby store. She will have to use the restroom in the second store and you can take the scanner to the sporting goods aisle. When she looks at the list online, you can feign ignorance. You won't get any of those items anyway; I didn't.

As you walk around the store, you are going to invariably run into other couples. You are about to enter into a fraternity that includes every dad on the planet. Give the other guys a knowing nod of the head; they would rather be watching games too. Eventually you will be talking with other dads about bowel movements, so you might as well start the kinship now. Guys would prefer registering at Home Depot or Champs, but they don't do that for babies (only bridal registries): "My kid could really use a 19.6 volt rechargeable hammer drill and a throwback Steelers jersey."

TEAM SHOWERS

Couples baby showers are a staple for today's dads. You will have to endure at least one. They aren't as bad as most people think. Try to plan this for a Tuesday or Wednesday night, if possible. Gathering around the living room of your closest friend with many people that care about your new little wide receiver is fun. You are going to open lots of presents and listen to everyone ooh and aah. I had season tickets to the Tampa Bay Bucs in the early 1990s. If I could sit through that, you can sit through a baby shower. (By the way, I refuse to dress my baby in bright orange because of scars on my psyche.)

You will survive one weekend of registering for baby stuff. Think of it as a rite of passage into the dad fraternity, kind of like rush week. Once you sit through a couples baby shower and spend a few days in the maternity ward, your initiation will be complete. You ought to get a pin or a sweatshirt once the initiation is over. You are now ready for training camp to get serious.

THE LOCKER ROOM

The thought of having a little one is probably sinking in as you approach the opening kickoff. You might have an occasional fumble as you approach D day, but you are probably still experiencing smooth sailing. You are dealing with the impending start of fatherdom. Registering is done and gifts will roll in as D day approaches. It is now time to start nesting for the baby.

Where does she go? How much space does she need? Will my old electric football game make a good changing table? How long does she sleep in our room? Do we try the family bed? These are all questions that you and your teammate have to discuss during training camp.

With a first child, you just have to face facts: You are going to lose a room originally intended for another purpose. If you are a professional athlete or a rock star, maybe this isn't the case. Since most of us can't run a 4.4 forty, hit a curveball, make a 32-foot jumper, sing like Nat King Cole, or drive a golf ball 300 yards, we are going to give something up. A spare bedroom, the office, the game room, and the media room are usually the first casualties. Decisions on each of these must be made on a case-by-case basis. If you live in a one-room studio, you might need to start hunting for a bigger stadium.

PLAYBOOK PAGE FOR REGISTERING

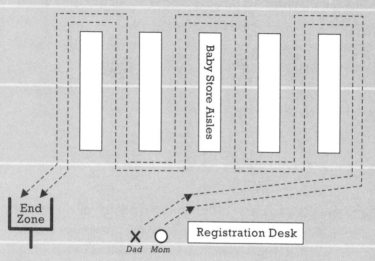

Baby Store Aisles

End Zone

✗ ○
Dad Mom

Registration Desk

Research big items before you go to the store to register.

Safety is the number one concern in big items.

Strollers come in many sizes and shapes; try a travel system.

Registration is an OTA.

Budget at least one full day and possibly two.

Registering is a rite of passage into the dad fraternity.

Snaps are required on all clothing until age three.

You might be in the market for a bigger stadium as the superstar arrives. If she is your first, find a house in which the master bedroom and the nursery are located close together. Remember, she will be up often and you will probably be the midnight delivery man after she is in her own room. Our master is on the first floor and the nursery is on the second; I stumbled up the stairs many times to bring my little superstar to the sidelines for a splash of milk. The split bedroom concept is good for teens; for newborns it is not.

A FAMILY LOCKER ROOM

A recommendation is that the baby rooms with you for several months. You can use a bassinet, cradle, or Moses basket. All three provide a comfortable place to sleep with close proximity to the milk truck. Once you learn how to swaddle a baby (a skill all QB dads should learn), you will realize they could sleep in a cardboard box. They will be unable to move.

Some people choose to sleep with the new star right in bed with them. This is known as the family bed. While this can be convenient for midnight milk refuels, you should consider all that this entails. Will you and your teammate lie awake all night for fear of rolling over and squishing your star, or will every little sound she makes cause you to think your star is in danger? The possibility of the family bed for a newborn might be risky. Many experts say no to the family bed for the first six months for safety. You and your teammate should decide what you feel most comfortable with. And, as always, talk to your pediatrician.

Another option is to use one crib that bolts to the side of your regular bed. These are called sidecar beds. If you are in the market for new bedroom furniture or plan on multiple draft picks, this might be worth the investment. They are safer than letting her sleep between you. The little superstar is going to be up every three hours anyway, so she needs to be close.

Touchdown

 Your little star will be up every three hours anyway, so she needs to be close.

Our little quarterback spent six months in a bassinet in our room before she went to her own locker room. After two months of nightly trips up the stairs and both teammates being exhausted, we decided on letting her sleep with us. Experts call this *reactive co-sleeping*. Experts have names for everything.

As you talk to other new dads, you may be surprised to find out family beds are more common than most people realize. Humans are probably the only animal that sends their young off to sleep by themselves (at least that is what my dear, wonderful, loving head coach tells me). Your parents will probably be mortified, but she is your little superstar. If you ask a dozen people, you will get a dozen different reasons and rationales why their way is best. This is a choice that you and your head coach have to make and be comfortable with.

If she moves to your bed, there are a few things to think about. Co-sleeping puts the infant at risk if the parents have impaired arousal from drug or alcohol use, or if a parent is obese. Parents who smoke may increase the child's risk for SIDS by co-sleeping. You also must have appropriate rails for the bed, just as with a crib, to keep the infant within the space without risk of getting stuck if she falls. Experts warn against putting babies on anything other than firm bedding, so make sure you have a firm mattress—no waterbeds or cheap foam mattresses. You also don't want any pillows or comforters close to her. She still must sleep on her back. Oh, and she will also sleep at right angles to you and the head coach. You need to get used to sleeping on your side on the last twelve inches of the mattress. And babies often talk in their sleep.

Moving her from a family bed back to a baby bed will take some extra work when you decide to do it. And sex with the head coach will take more creativity, but that can actually be fun. You might need to tiptoe to other rooms, or use the floor.

This still doesn't get you out of the nursery debate. After all, you need someplace to put all the 2,000 things that you will get for her. Let's examine a few potential rooms to use for the locker room (nursery).

LOCKER ROOM CHOICES

The choice of giving up a spare bedroom is based on your own personal needs. Do you have lots of family living at far distances? Remember that in-laws and parents are actually encouraged to visit after the little prospect is here. They are a tremendous help and are cheaper than baby sitters. How long they stay is going to depend on how comfortable they are. I get along great with my in-laws, but for some people that isn't the case. If you want their stay to be short, make them uncomfortable—think fold-out couches. But this is a wonderful time to bond with your teammate's mother and your own mother. Encourage them to stay and help out. Ask for advice; just remember it's your little linebacker and you can ignore their advice.

 *The new nursery is the **locker room** for your little star.*

The locker room can always double as a guest room if you just put a normal-size bed in the room. The crib can be tucked against one wall, and the little one will sleep in your room for a few months anyway. You can even keep the bed in the locker room as your little one becomes a veteran. Once they are older, most children don't mind being kicked out of their bedrooms; sleeping on the floor in the game room is a treat. The crib is a great storage place to store baby gifts since your star won't need it initially.

 *The crib is also a great storage place to store shower gifts until you open boxes and remove price tags. Think of the crib as a **sideline equipment table**.*

You can also combine a spare bedroom and an office, which will free up a room. If you work out of your home and have a real office, this isn't always possible. For at least a year, combining the office and nursery is a definite possibility.

But unless you are moving to a bigger stadium in that year, you might want to relocate the office to a more permanent space.

Our office moved into the breakfast nook as we prepared for the start of the regular season. Besides, you don't need a designated space just to eat Pop Tarts. This actually means we now use our dining room. It seems odd most people (in a house) have a dining room and almost never use it. If space is tight, you can also use your master bedroom as an office. They make computer armoires that close up to hide everything the typical home office has.

A game or media room can be converted into a nursery. If you have both in your house, you could combine the two. Keep the game/media room but babyproof it (more on babyproofing the house in Chapter 11). Good selling point to your partner: This room will make the perfect play place later in life. Besides, once the little quarterback is here, you won't be able to go out at the spur of the moment anyway. You need a room that is designed for relaxation and the baby is free to roam in.

Touchdown

Try to resist the urge to give up your game or media room.

For about the first six months, the baby will stay exactly where you place her. She may roll over, but that will be it. After that, she will be all over the place. Having at least one room to watch games and feel confident the baby is safe is perfect. A pool table is just the right height to change a baby on; just make sure that you put a waterproof changing pad down first. Now you have the perfect reason to lobby your teammate for a pool table. I have actually changed my baby on a pinball machine and I didn't need a changing pad.

LOCKER ROOM GEAR

The furniture needed in a baby locker room is important. From cribs to dressers and everything in between, you won't believe how much gear is needed for one tiny star.

Cribs

An adjustable crib is critical, because she will start climbing after the first year. The mattress can be lowered as she gets older, making it more difficult for her to reach the top. Cribs with drop-down sides are ideal if one of you is short in stature. The drop-down sides will allow almost any height person to lay the baby down safely.

Fumble *An adjustable crib is critical, because as she ages she will turn into Sir Edmund Hilary, the first guy to reach the summit of Mount Everest.*

They also make convertible cribs that sound good in theory. It is a crib that can be converted to a toddler bed when the baby is ready. They even make models that will then convert into a full-size bed with a headboard. We bought a convertible crib, but it probably won't survive to the headboard stage.

Besides, they make toddler beds for almost every cute cartoon character that your star will fall in love with. The same mattress will work in both the crib and the toddler bed.

Equipment Lockers

You need an equipment locker to fill with all of her clothes. An equipment locker is just a fun name for a dresser. To guys, a dresser is any piece of furniture for a bedroom that contains more than two drawers. To the head coach, the dresser is the long, short one; the tall one is called a chest. The short dresser is the safest because it won't tip over very easily. But your star will eventually be able to get in every drawer. You might want at least one drawer they can't reach until they are five for storage of small stuff. The tall dresser will fill this need. If you only get one for the baby, tall is the way to go.

Tape Tables

All locker rooms have a table to lay on while you get your ankles taped for the big game. All nurseries have a changing table. A changing table is necessary for obvious reasons. They come in every variety: stand-alone, built into the dresser, and a changing pad that fits on any furniture. I lost a close one-to-one vote on using a 1970s electric football table as a changing table. We opted for a regular dresser and a separate changing pad that can be removed when no longer needed. She probably won't potty train until she is at least two years old, so this pad will be well used.

THE LOCKER ROOM

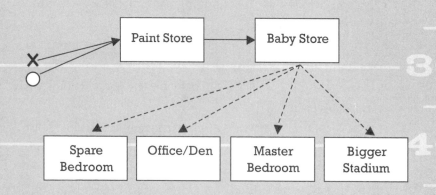

You are going to have to choose a room for the baby.

The baby will probably share your room for the first few months.

Co-sleeping is more common than you realize.

Try to keep a family room, playroom, or media room for when your star is older.

Buy an adjustable crib.

Attach all furniture to the wall.

The crib is a great storage place for gifts, until it is needed.

For safety purposes, secure all dressers and the changing table to the wall. Your star will eventually pull out drawers and try to climb. Some kids don't climb much, but most try it a few times. My daughter is a daredevil; she scales everything like a monkey. The changing pad must also be secured to the table or dresser. The changing pad has a belt on it and should be used from diaper one. Place all needed diaper supplies within arm's reach so you don't have to move to get something. Never leave the baby on the pad without you standing over her.

The locker room needs a decorating theme. You can shoot for a sports-themed room, but be prepared to lose any one-to-one votes again. The head coach gets the nod on any tie-breakers, since she will go through excruciating contortions to bring your draft pick into the world. Decorate the locker room early in pregnancy with your teammate and have fun.

Make the room bright, fun, and colorful. You can paint the walls neutral and liven it up with accessories, or paint with the most outrageous colors. Bright colors are supposedly the best to stimulate your little star as she develops. You can go into any baby store and find complete matched theme sets. All manner of curtains, crib stuff, and accessories will already be coordinated for you. Like deciding whether to go on a fourth down, this choice will most likely be made by the head coach. My advice on choosing a theme is "Yes, Dear."

Choosing and preparing the locker room for your future star will get you closer to draft day. Training camp is in full swing now.

SAVING MONEY
WITHOUT SCALPING
4. YOUR SEATS

As your family grows, it is time to sit down with the head coach and discuss finances. Your little superstar is going to cost extra money; there is no way around that. Money is never fun to discuss, but you must plan for a new baby. Financial decisions are important as you adjust to a bigger team.

All of us have various degrees of income and money savvy. A little planning and belt tightening will go a long way to helping your team run smoothly. Since the baby is the team owner, shouldn't he be in charge of finances? In some cases, the baby might do better than we do.

Does anybody ever have enough money? It seems like the more we have, the more we want. Well, we have to face facts. Most of us aren't as talented as our sports heroes. We don't get long-term, big-money contracts. Maybe a few of you are making a living at playing football. Congratulations. But most of us are more like interior offensive linemen: doing a day's work for a day's pay.

We don't have shoe contracts and endorsement deals. In most cases, it was our parent's fault. If I had been taller, faster, and able to throw a deep out, I would be playing the game I love instead of coaching it. I love my parents deeply, but I wish Dad was taller, faster, and even that he had more hair. Oops, he is taller, faster, and has more hair than me. I also wish he had bought Apple stock in 1980, but who knew? You can't pick your parents. You just love the ones you have.

Fumble *Everybody would like more money, but more money usually means more bills.*

You might get a signing bonus for your new superstar. Think of the cash and gift cards that you get for your new baby as a signing bonus. This can be spent for any purpose. Of course, it is meant for the baby. And wouldn't you and the star look great in matching Steelers jerseys? And wouldn't Disney movies look better on a big-screen TV?

N F L *The **signing bonus** is the combination of cash and gift cards that you get for your new superstar.*

The cost of raising a newborn through college age is estimated at anywhere from ten to fifteen thousand dollars a year. This cost seems high to me, but those are the numbers bandied about by experts. To cover the costs of raising your superstar, you and the head coach will make some tough decisions.

FINANCIAL PLANNING

Communication between the QB dad and the head coach is always important, but money matters are of primary importance.

You both need to openly discuss what you want for your team. Financial planning is not fun or glamorous; it is more like film study for an upcoming opponent. It is necessary and will make your game plan run smoother. Just like in an actual game, there will be wrinkles. Planning ahead of time will make these wrinkles easier to deal with.

One Income or Two

The first major decision that all new parents have to make is one income or two. And usually this comes down to a lifestyle choice. You have to take an honest look at what you value. Is having a stay-at-home parent worth the sacrifice? The lifestyle that you want usually comes down to wants and needs. It is important to know the difference. Needs are food, shelter, and clothing. Wants are everything else.

The importance of having a stay-at-home parent is a personal choice. The choice is not as dependent on money as you may think. But to go from two salaries to one will take sacrifices. Are you willing to drive an older car? Willing to watch games from a recliner that has been repaired with duct tape? Willing to stay in your cramped locker room? All of these choices play a role in your decision.

Touchdown

Living on one income is a choice, but it is a difficult financial choice.

Choices lead many of us to increase our bills to maintain a lifestyle that often is for other people's benefit. Keeping up with the Joneses is a common and all too often true statement. We buy a new car to enhance our prestige in the parking lot. Perhaps you can drive an old car and park around the corner. We want the newest shoes, hiking gear, retro jerseys, and a fancier house. Most of the budget busters are really just wants, not needs.

A larger house (and the mortgage payment) is a want and not always a need. Most people can think back to some time in their lives (growing up, college years, the newlywed years) when they lived off a lot less money. That proves that it is possible. You will need to prioritize what you spend money on.

Can you afford to maintain your prestar lifestyle on only one person's salary? If you can, that is fantastic. You can actually try this during training camp. Try to bank one entire salary for three months and live off of the other salary. Even if you find out this doesn't work, you may have built a nice beginning to a college fund. And today it seems like college costs are rising faster than NFL salaries.

 Staying home with a child is not all soap operas and long
Fumble *naps, but it could be* **SportsCenter** *and long naps.*

In addition to money, you have to think about if either of you truly want to stay home. I have many friends who say they are better parents because they both work. Staying home is hard work, not all *SportsCenter* and long naps. There are many days that most stay-at-home parents would rather be punching a time clock.

A stay-at-home parent even requires more work than many jobs. It can be a very rewarding job, but it is a job! No hiding in your cubicle when the baby calls. The stay-at-home choice is a team decision because it will affect both of your lifestyles. Downsizing is a choice that many couples opt for, but it is a choice that you both make and live with.

Having one of you stay home for a smaller, fixed amount of time may be a compromise. Decide on one year (or some other set time) and try. Of course, you have to be confident that you can get a job when the time is up. Many companies will offer a leave of absence for up to a year for family reasons. It might be easier to budget if you know living on one income is only going to be for a fixed length of time.

There are also ways that a stay-at-home parent can earn extra money. These include watching another child, direct-marketing schemes, and part-time jobs. More and more companies will allow you to cut back and work at home. Part-time work at home with a baby takes careful scheduling and maximum efficiency.

QB dads can always rent out the kid to their single guy friends. Single guys with babies will attract women like flies to honey. But the friend has to be worthy enough to be trusted with your little star. And if they would rent your kid to pick up women, they are not. Of course, you could go with them and supervise, but people might assume he is already taken. Well, it was a good thought, but I wouldn't try it.

Why Do You Work?

A very important question for you and the head coach to answer is why you work. Is your job a calling? Is it something that you are compelled to do? This is a personal decision, but it needs to be discussed with the head coach. She also needs to examine and share her reasons for working.

You can raise a child well on two salaries or one. The four pivotal questions to answer are:

1. Can you afford it?
2. Is it worth the sacrifice?
3. Is one of you willing?
4. Is one of you capable of doing it?

Either way, changes will probably have to be made. Some are easy, some are harder. But if one of you stays home, bigger cuts need to be made. Look for obvious things you can eliminate. Can you replace your gym membership with daily stroller walks? Can you survive with only one car or no car at all? Do you have enough relatives willing to feed you once a week? Do you have a friend with a large-screen television for bowl games and the Super Bowl?

EXPENSES

Usually rent or mortgage and utilities are somewhat fixed amounts. Many other monthly expenses aren't fixed. Where can you trim money? Can you cut back on your cell phone bill? Can you get rid of your home phone entirely? Many people already have with the convenience of cell phones. Can you carpool or take mass transit, shop at cheaper places for food, drink wine out of a box, buy domestic beer, or get cheaper seats at the stadium?

The largest discretionary item in a budget for many people is entertainment. Are movies, shows, and dining out that important? Trimming one or two restaurant meals a month will add up quick. Of course, this saved money will probably be blown on diapers and wipes.

Entertainment

Entertainment once you have a child can get more expensive, because now you have to find a baby sitter. You still need to go out occasionally for your own sanity. Maybe you can trade baby-sitting with a friend who also has a baby. In addition, all people have several baby lovers among their circle of friends. You might try short dinners out while they watch your star. If your parents/in-laws live close, they love spoiling their grand-superstar. Baby sitters are like backup quarterbacks: the most popular person around.

Touchdown

Some of your fun money will be redistributed from seven-course meals to baby sitters.

I can't believe I am going to say this, but here it goes: You can watch games on TV instead of actually going to the stadium. That hurts me to put that into print. I have made a few sacrifices: I no longer drink eight-dollar beers and eat four-dollar hot dogs at games. I fill up at the tailgate parties first.

Just wait until your little star is old enough to go and enjoy the games. Then you can call it quality time. There is nothing like the bonding experience of booing the referees together.

And you can hide food in the diaper bag. The security guards will search the bag, but the baby has to eat. In the next few years, you are going to eat a lot of animal crackers and carrot sticks. They are both cheaper than four-dollar hot dogs.

Baby Clothing

Name-brand clothing is an extravagance for new babies. My motto is "No logos until she asks for them." And trust me, she *will* ask and it will be sooner than you want. Logos drive up the price of clothes and shoes. A pair of brand-name shoes for a kid is a pure want. Your star doesn't even need shoes for almost a year, although the head coach might want one pair to bronze as a keepsake.

When she is in elementary school (or maybe earlier), peer pressure will start and they will want certain logos; you will have to learn to tell your kid no. Fifty-dollar shoes are still just shoes. No kid needs name-brand shoes or clothes, but most will eventually want name brands.

Touchdown

 All QB dads must buy outfits that show off their favorite team.

The one logo exception for all QB dads is the favorite team sleeper or onesie. You might actually need two, one for your favorite pro team and one for the college team. By the way, the team sleeper is a need, not a want. All QB dads are required to dress their star in the team colors. If you are not shy about your favorite teams, these will probably come as gifts.

Also, the head coach may insist on onesies for her favorite team.

Most people (me included) have way more clothes for their star than the star can wear. We have outfits that may never be worn, because junior will outgrow them first. Never turn down any offered hand-me-downs is my advice. You will get new outfits or ones that have only been worn once. After one washing, your new outfits will look the same anyway.

Baby Needs

Buying store-brand diapers is a way to save cash. You might have to experiment with different types for the best fit. Expensive diapers will soak up baby poop just like the cheaper ones. And they are probably made in the same plant, just on the night shift.

In my experience, store-brand wipes seem to wipe a butt as good as the expensive ones. Also, buy in bulk for all of the above. The two-hands-to-carry box of diapers is cheaper per poop than smaller packages. You can buy the cute little plastic tubs of wipes and then fill them with refill packs that come six to a box. If you use cloth diapers, compare different services to see which has the best deal.

To save money on detergent, buy the store-brand dye- and perfume-free detergent in the bigger bottle. A well-known baby laundry detergent is almost four times the cost of the cheap stuff. In my unofficial tests, they both clean up baby spit-up equally well. Remember, your laundry amount will triple when the house grows in size. Be aware that the head coach can and will supersede you in these decisions.

WAYS TO MAKE THE BABY PAY

Watching the Large Delivery Company Fiesta Bowl hosted by Large Snack Company at the Latest Mega-Telecom Bowl last New Year's Day gave me an idea. Pregame shows, postgame shows, stadiums, and halftimes are all for sale. Why can't I name everything affiliated with my daughter in exchange for dollars? I have tried Boudreaux Butt Paste Changing Table and the Pampers Diaper Pail, but the companies have not agreed to any deals . . . yet.

 Contact all of the major sneaker companies and agree to a **Fumble** *lifetime deal in exchange for free clothes and shoes.*

Another option would be to contact all of the major sneaker companies and agree to a lifetime deal in exchange for free clothes and shoes. This would only cost you money if your kid becomes the next Peyton Manning.

One guaranteed way to offset the cost of your star is investing in stocks of companies whose products you will use. Buy stock in your favorite battery brand. You will go through 13,512 batteries for all of the toys that she will acquire over the first ten years of her life. Also buy stock in your favorite baby food company. Babies have to eat and play; might as well make some money along the way. Buy stock in the company that produces your head coach's stain remover. The head coach will buy stain remover every time she goes to the store after the baby is born.

Experts say that most couples fight about money and sex. With a newborn in the house, sex may be a distant memory,

SCALPING YOUR SEATS TO THE BIG GAME

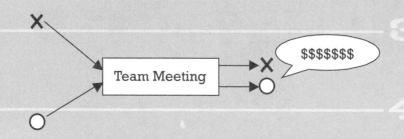

Communication about money is vital between the parents.

Decide on one income or two.

Being a stay-at-home parent is hard work.

Going out once you have a child gets more expensive.

Name-brand clothing is an extravagance for new babies.

Buy stock in your favorite battery brand and baby food company.

Set up regular team meetings to discuss money.

but money decisions will have to be made. Communication is the key. Decide what you value and want as a team. A periodic team meeting on money will keep you on the same page. All good football staffs meet to communicate goals. Your staff needs to meet also.

Touchdown

Buy stock in battery, baby food, and stain remover companies now.

PUTTING A NAME
5. ON THE UNIFORM

Nicole, Megan, Zebulon, James, John, Paul, George, Ringo . . . how *do* you pick a name? Naming your baby will take more mental energy in the months leading up to the birth than any physics test you took in college. Of course, the baby already has a team name (your last name), but the decision on the first name is all important.

Well, the last name is usually a given, but not always. The last name in some cases can cause an argument between the QB dad and the head coach. As people choose not to marry, or marry later, the last name may be up for debate. Dad's name usually wins, but not always. You can always choose the boardroom merger approach, like Morgan Stanley Dean Witter. Hyphenated names are more commonplace. If your child was conceived at work, this may be perfect. Don't all guys have the office fantasy?

The first name you choose will have a lasting effect on your child, so choose wisely. Choosing a bad name forces your child to deal with a life of abuse, or at least the first few years in school. In my years of teaching, I saw some strange names. Aquanet and Aquanetta were students of mine in back-to-back years and weren't even related. My all-time favorite student name has to be Phuc, a bright, engaging child who insisted I call him Jimmy. I had never been so happy to oblige a student's wish.

Picking a name will be compounded if you elect not to find out the sex because you have to choose two names. Deciding on two names just increases the mental energy you expend, but it is not the end of the world. Be prepared with a boy and girl name when you set off to the hospital. Pick out a name (or two) before you get to the hospital. If you know the sex, still decide before you get to draft day.

Fumble *Don't decide on a name at the hospital; get it done ahead of time. A head coach doesn't decide the first play of the game after kickoff.*

Of course, if you find out the sex, you can line up a name and prepare. Don't tell people the name ahead of time if you tell people the sex. Otherwise, when you tell people "the baby is here," they won't have much to ask.

Have a backup name in case your John turns out to be a Johanna. You can wait up to three days in most states before you have to officially decide on the name. Don't do that to your kid (unless the head coach insists).

As you debate names, pretend you are in the third grade again and try to find as many ways to pick on the name as possible. If you find more than one way to butcher a name, suggest another. I wouldn't recommend buying a book of names either (although the head coach might not give you a choice). With the Internet, lists of names are easy to come by and you will save a few coins. Besides, most people with a book end up with a child's name that begins with A through D, because they tire of reading it.

 Don't choose a name that can easily be rhymed with **Fumble** *something demeaning.*

Family names are a nice way to honor somebody but just as easily can make somebody else mad. Look at your family tree for people with money to honor. If you are going to honor someone, it might as well be someone with cash. When choosing a family name of a living relative, you will make one person very happy but you may disappoint several.

Many dads insist on naming their star after themselves. This is a purely personal choice, but prepare for some difficulties. How are you going to differ between the two of you? "Junior" is one way to tell the difference. Or one of you can go by a middle name or permanent nickname. This is probably easy when you are a kid, but it might be harder when official mail comes to the house for both of you. I coached with a father-son combo set. Dad is Charlie and the son is Bubba, but only to his family. You guessed it; he is Charlie to everybody else. Nobody ever knew which one we were talking about at staff meetings.

CUTTING NAMES

You only get one vote, but you can eliminate some names from contention that you don't like. There are a few ways to do this.

If you are having a girl, you can get rid of names by playing the old girlfriend card. She wants April and you hate the name, just say "I had an old girlfriend named April" and that name is off the list. My head coach eliminated a name I liked for a girl by playing the pet card. We now have a cat named Molly.

For boys' names, you can play the archenemy ploy. When she suggests Bruce, say "I hated Bruce when I was in the third grade." This can cover at least six or seven grades, more if you graduated high school at twenty-three.

Touchdown

Research what other names are popular at the time to avoid your little star having to include an initial on her jersey. It's not quite as fun cheering, "Run, Katie L!"

You can see what names are popular by going to the Social Security Web site (*www.socialsecurity.gov/OACT/babynames/*). This can prevent your boy from being in a kindergarten class with seven other Christophers. I taught a high-school class of twenty students that contained four Ryans one year. I know what the most popular name was sixteen years before that class. Names also run in cycles, and we are currently seeing a resurgence of old names again.

Nicknames

There has also been a move away from short nicknames over the last ten years. Today, James is James, not Jim or Jimmy or Jimbo. That is not a major problem, but thirty years ago almost everyone had a shorter nickname. The IRS calls me Robert, but everyone else calls me Bobby. Well, a few call me Bob and many call me names that are inappropriate for this book. If your kid becomes famous, a nickname can make him stand out, even if the name never appears on his birth certificate. Booger, Scooter, and Pork Chop are all examples of this. If your kid becomes really famous, he won't even need your last name. Think Madonna, Peyton, and Tiger.

Creative Spellings

Spell your kid's name any way you want, but make sure you are prepared. If you choose a nontraditional way of spelling, problems might ensue.

Fumble *Different spellings will make their Christmas stocking harder to fill.*

Different spellings will cause problems for small gifts. You will never find pencils, note pads, magnets, or stickers that contain the different spelling. My wife Michele (with one L) even had a college professor who called her "One L." By all means, if you have a last name that will always have to be spelled, don't saddle the kid with a first name like that too. Don't pair Edquisha with a last name like Canamucio.

Cute Names

Cute names at the time may end up sounding silly in the future. I played softball many years ago with a guy who had a brother named Cash Register on his birth certificate. I have a distant cousin named Candy Kane. Imagine the abuse she had to endure on the playground. I overheard a mother call her child by name not too long ago. When I asked her to repeat it, she just started laughing and said it was her husband's idea. The boy's name was Espn. Now that is a serious QB dad. You can try that name if you have a big enough set of stones.

In the free democratic society that we live in, you only get one vote. Be prepared; you will very possibly lose any one-to-one votes with your spouse. Try very hard to eliminate really harsh names. Just like lawyers picking jurors at a trial, you can probably get rid of a few without cause. To eliminate more than three or four, try the girlfriend/archenemy ploy. Remember, your kid will live with that name longer than you will.

Touchdown

You only get one vote in picking a name and that vote can be vetoed by the head coach.

The bags are packed, the nursery is painted, the car is full of gas, and your teammate is as big as a house (but more beautiful than ever). Training camp is coming to a close; you are now ready for the preseason.

PUTTING A NAME ON THE UNIFORM

"Peyton, LeBron, Tiger ..."

X

"Matthew, James, Phillip ..."

O

EXTRA POINTS

The name you choose will have a lasting effect on your child, so choose wisely.

Finding out the sex is a purely private decision, so don't bend to pressure.

Don't decide at the hospital; get it done ahead of time.

Have a backup name in case Christopher turns out to be a Christine.

Don't choose a name that can easily be rhymed with something demeaning.

If you are having a girl, you can get rid of names by playing the old girlfriend card.

For boys names, you can play the archenemy ploy.

Cute names at the time may end up sounding silly in the future.

HEADSETS AND
6. GAME PLANS

Scripts, hit sheets, game plans, play sheets—they have many names. I am talking about those laminated, color-coded, legal-sized sheets of paper that you see most coaches carrying as they prowl the sidelines.

In the television age, these sheets have become more noticeable. No longer are they rolled up in a back pocket or on the clipboard at waist level. These game plans are now used by coaches to foil lip readers watching a television feed.

Today's coaches leave nothing to chance, and neither should you as you prepare for D day. Game plans are broken down for special situations: what to call on first and ten, third and three, two-minute situations, two-point plays.

game plan: *the birth plan of how your number one draft pick will enter the world.*

In baby terms, a game plan is called a birth plan. How your little star will come into the world needs to be part of your birth plan. You will huddle with the head coach to make most of these decisions, but she will get the ultimate nod on most of these. You may also just be handed the game plan and have zero input. Some head coaches don't want any input. The game plan is important and should be shared with all of the important people. But the game plan also needs to be flexible.

DRAFT DAY LOCATION

First of all, you need to choose where to have the baby. Choices are a hospital, birthing center, at home, or the backseat of a taxi. Hospitals are the most common choice here. Today's maternity wards are much more luxurious and friendly than the place you and I entered the world in. A hospital comes equipped with all the extras to prepare for any emergency. Hospitals are usually the one place that will provide epidurals, and that is often the deciding factor.

Most birthing centers are like minihospitals. They most likely have a nursery, pediatrician on site, and many trained experts. They just won't have old guys getting bypasses right next door. Many are not equipped for C-sections or epidurals, so if those are on the plan you need to head for the regular hospital. All birth centers should have an agreement with a full-service hospital for quick transport if the need arises. Most birth centers will send you home within twenty-four hours, so be prepared if you go that route.

Of course, having a baby at your home is also an option. With a trusted midwife, this option will probably run smooth. Midwives are usually very experienced and prepared for most options. Diagnostic machines are better at determining many potential problems ahead of time nowadays. You will probably be instructed to go to a hospital/birthing center if any problems are found ahead of time.

The back of a taxi would be the least desirable place to bring your new draft pick into the world. But a birth plan, like a game plan, sometimes has to be adjusted as the game progresses. Nobody plans for the back of a taxi.

PREGAME WALK-THROUGH

Prepare for your drive to the hospital by mapping out the best route and prepacking the car. It might be a good idea to drive it at several different times during the day to get your timing down. Coaches practice, and dads should too. Go to the hospital and find out what to do when you get there. Hopefully, you have already had a hospital tour and have been given the ground rules. You can always enter through the emergency room. Nurses in the ER will get you out fast; they don't want to deliver babies anymore than you do.

Touchdown

Take a hospital tour with the head coach.
Do not wait until the last minute.

As you approach the due date, make sure the car is continuously gassed up. Keep an eye on the weather if it is winter or hurricane season. As you reach the promised delivery date, you might want to spend the night with relatives or friends depending on your distance to the hospital.

For the last month, move the passenger seat as far back as possible and empty the back seat. I had a friend who went to the hospital on her hands and knees in the backseat. Laying the front seat back might also help buy you a few minutes to get to the hospital. You are going to need to get the seat in the most comfortable position possible.

PACKING FOR DRAFT DAY

My head coach is organized in the personal packing department. Funny thing, my wife and I didn't pack at all. My wife had something called a cephalopelvic disproportion, which means there is a good chance the baby's head is larger than the opening. For safety reasons, the doctors suggested a C-section and it was already scheduled for a Tuesday. No need to pack early, or so we thought. We had a long talk Friday night about what to pack on Saturday morning. We also discussed going out to eat and a movie that weekend for our last pregame date.

But as they say, the best laid plans. . . . At 6:30 Saturday morning, I was awakened to the words "Oh @%$#" as my wife jumped out of bed. Her water had broke. I was going to be a dad sometime that day. I flew about the bedroom as if I was down by three points with thirty seconds left in the game. I grabbed clothes for her from the maternity stack and started tossing them in our bag. I was scrambling like I was being chased. My wife was surprisingly calm as she laughed at my clothing choices for her. I can still hear the words "I am not wearing *that* in public." Panic mode is common for dads on this day . . . you are allowed.

Treat the hospital stay like it is the first preseason game of the year. You want to make a good impression for your legions of adoring fans (and the head coach). Your partner might have already packed a bag for herself and your little prospect.

As a backup plan, give a house key to a trusted friend so he can sneak out and get anything you forgot. Think of this friend (or family member) as your backup quarterback: on the sidelines wearing a baseball hat but ready if needed.

 The **backup quarterback** *is a friend who is prepared to bring anything you forgot to the hospital.*

For dads, it is a good idea to bring your own pillow, comfortable clothes and shoes, favorite team hat, cell phone charger, phone list, camera, extra film, extra batteries, a hazmat suit, and some type of nonperishable edible food. Any of the major snack cakes fall into the nonperishable category. Twinkies, Ho-Hos, and Ding Dongs are never going to mold or go bad. Trust me; snack cakes will survive the next giant asteroid. You can even place all this stuff in the car as you near draft day.

 Pack snack cakes in your hospital bag; they never go bad.
Fumble

You want comfortable shoes and clothes because you may be in them for twenty or more hours straight. You might be able to sneak in a shower in the middle of delivery, but it is doubtful. The hazmat suit will be needed once you enter the delivery room. You may also want to get a haircut, and you should shave often in the last few days before draft day. On draft day you will be in hundreds of pictures with your number one draft pick, so you want to look nice. These pictures will be seen for dozens of years.

You might also want to load up the car with clean towels and hot boiling water in case you have to deliver the baby. Just kidding . . . I hope. Having babies in cars is much more common on television than in real life. Since that appears to be true, by all means, do not let a television station document the birth or you could end up being the dad and a doctor.

PLAY CALLS ON THE HEADSET

Your cell phone will serve as a QB dad's headset on game day. Keep the headset charged as draft day approaches. If your battery is weak, grab a cell phone from your teammate. Always remember to bring your cell phone charger to the game.

 Cell phones are the **headset** *for the QB dad.*

The friend and distant family phone list is also important. Prepare it ahead of time and have the head coach look it over. Put it in your wallet (or somewhere equally sacred). The head coach might also just hand you a list to check. Prioritize the list based on importance and how sensitive each person is. Family tops the list. They will always be around and might not be willing to forgive. You should call both sets of soon-to-be-grandparents first, maybe even in the car on the way to the hospital. Or call them once your teammate is through the

HEADSETS AND GAMEPLANS

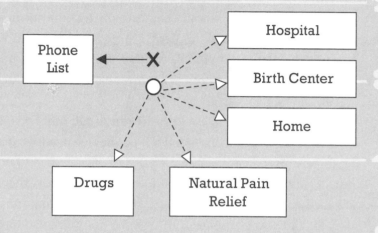

A game plan is the birth plan for how your star will enter the world.

Some head coaches aren't going to want any input from you.

Hospital, birth centers, and home are options for where the head coach gives birth.

Decide on the pain-relief method (for the head coach).

Prioritize a phone list of who to call in correct order.

Keep the cell phone fully charged and in your pocket.

Get as much sleep as possible; you may be awake for hours in the hospital.

door. They will understand if you can't talk. They can start a phone tree to tell the rest of the family.

You can also phone tree your friends. The first guy you should tell is your best friend. With most men, the list of intimate friends is short, so call them personally. I'm not talking about tailgating buddies here. I am talking about those few friends that wouldn't make you pay back a five hundred dollar bet on the Super Bowl. The ones that understand that sometimes you get carried away.

You may also want to ask a few friends to call other people after the fact. It isn't a big deal if the phone tree overlaps; better for friends to hear the news from three people than to not hear it at all. Many people will understand if you miss them. For the people that won't understand, decide how important they are in the big scheme of things. On draft day, you have far more important things to worry about.

Touchdown

Keep the headset charged fully as draft day approaches.

The game plan and the headset will help you have a smoother time as the day approaches. You have crossed midfield and are on your way to being a dad. Relax and try to get a few last good nights of sleep. Eight straight hours of sleep will not occur for the next six months. Some people say that you can rest in the hospital. Well, not in my experience. Not when you come home with your star either. Matter of fact, put the book down and go to bed now. Tell the head coach you are going to dream of her.

7. DRAFT DAY

First and goal at the two yard line. You are about to become a QB dad. In a matter of hours, you are going to be holding your first-round draft pick. This will be one of the happiest moments of your life and also one of the most stressful. Enjoy the moment. Savor the sights, sounds, and feelings that you are having. Well, some sights might be best forgotten, but more on that later.

Your head coach's comfort is the number one priority as soon as you settle into the room. Trained people are going to be monitoring the situation; they are used to this. The only panic in the room will probably be from you. Odd that guys panic; your partner is doing all the hard stuff. But most of us panic nonetheless.

Touchdown

Keep the head coach happy and calm if possible.

Funny thing is, once you are at the hospital or birth center, panic time should be over. Once you are ensconced in a labor room, the staff is trained for every conceivable problem that could arise. Good thing, since you didn't really want to deliver the baby yourself. People had babies for thousands of years before they had hospitals, but I didn't have to live through that and neither do you. Progress is a good thing.

A major choice is drugs (for her, not you). My wife wanted an epidural the minute we walked through the door. An epidural will block off any feeling below the waist. Demerol and other similar drugs are often given as an assist during labor. She will still be able to push, but it will take the edge off of the pain. Contractions must hurt like hell. Your partner is not going to be rational when a contraction hits. Remember these words: "Yes, Dear." She may call you names, curse at you, and even threaten you with never having sex again. Most of these rants will be forgotten after Cletus leaves the womb.

Cletus has been comfortably ensconced in a fluid-filled sack for nine months but now has to get out. That sack rupturing is her water breaking. That is sometimes the first sign that Junior is on the way. It is also possible that the head coach will go into labor first and the doctors will have to break open the sack, but it usually breaks by itself. It is also possible that the water can break with her not being in labor at all.

She is about to deliver your first-round draft pick, and now is not the time for debate or humor. The next few hours and days are going to give you many things to laugh about, so you can wait until you're both comfortable for the jokes. Every dad has a funny delivery story. Many have several. Funny hospital stories are kind of like big-game stories. They are fun to talk about and can get passed down from generation to generation. And they may get embellished.

VAGINAL DELIVERIES

The most common births are of the good old-fashioned vaginal variety. With this type you will take a more prominent role. Matter of fact, you will gain the temporary title of coach. It's possible that your partner may have a doula or a midwife as the coach, but it is usually the dad. Your teammate will reclaim the title after your first-round draft pick has been unveiled. The vaginal delivery is usually a longer and more painful process than a C-section. At least it's more painful at the time.

Labor will usually start on its own with contractions. These contractions will get stronger and longer as the baby prepares for his debut. You will be responsible for comforting her and helping her breathe. I hope you were paying attention in breathing class. You also need to make sure she stays hydrated. Labor can last a very long time, especially with your first draft pick. Twenty hours is not uncommon. With second-round draft picks, the time will generally be less. The wife of a friend of mine delivered baby number two while he was parking the car.

Contractions will start slow, and you may be encouraged to walk around with your wife to let gravity help the process along. You will have to make sure she is as relaxed as possible and not pushing yet. Pushing early will usually extend the birth process. She will often be hooked up to a fetal monitor while all this is going on. The monitor looks like the same hookup that sports drink commercials show for athletes in training. Try to get her in a comfortable position. Standing, squatting, walking, and on all fours are the usual suspects.

The baby's head will be pushing at the opening, but the opening (cervix) will have to thin and stretch out. The doctors may administer a drug to help this process along.

When the last part of labor starts, the experts will tell her to push and help squeeze your little one out. This will be as hard for her as any weightlifting you have ever done.

One push won't do it; this can be a long process (up to one hour or longer). Keep her as relaxed as possible and tell her "I love you" every 2.9 seconds. She may threaten you with bodily harm, but tell her anyway.

The head will be the first part through in most deliveries (in a breech birth the feet will come out first). The shoulders will follow the head, and then your star is here. Celebrate with a little victory dance and then lean down and give the head coach a kiss. You lose the title of coach, but you will always be your draft pick's QB dad.

C-SECTIONS

The head coach's and the baby's health are the primary concerns. If there is any doubt about safety, doctors will recommend a cesarean section. Doctors would rather take a safe, controlled route if they anticipate any potential problems. A C-section is like punting on a fourth and one—the safe call. The doctors become the referees in this case and you could lose the ability to challenge.

My head coach had a C-section because they thought the baby was larger than the pelvic opening. Some women don't want a C-section under any circumstances. Remember, the doctors are professionals, and if they think it is best, go with their thoughts. If your wife begins to complain, calm her and listen to her. Don't argue with her. Once Cletus is out, it won't matter how Cletus got out. You will both be overjoyed. Once the decision is made to operate, they will move your partner to the surgery area.

Touchdown

 Regardless of how the baby gets out, you will both be ecstatic.

You are still needed to soothe your wife and possibly fill her in on what is happening. They will give her an epidural, which means she won't feel anything from the waist down. She will still be awake. When prepped, she will be draped in sheets and ready to go. They will roll her into the OR to deliver your little QB. All ORs look alike: lots of white tile and toothpaste-green walls.

BLOOD AND GUTS

I will admit that I am squeamish at the sight of blood. You can't have any type of delivery without blood. Joy. For my wife's C-section, I hid behind the green sheet that was draped across her chest. From there, I could see her and comfort her and take pictures. I never looked over the sheet; I had no desire to see my wife's internal plumbing.

Delivery rooms are full of bodily fluids and even a few solids as your little star comes into the world. Blood and amniotic fluid (broken water) are a given. There will also be afterbirth, which is the placenta. All of this mess is necessary to get Cletus out.

After the all-star arrives, the nurses and/or a pediatrician will examine the baby from head to toe and then whisk it off to the nursery. You have to leave your partner while she gets stitched up. Tell her you love her as you leave with your new star. She might forget all the pain, but she will never forget those three little words.

Fumble

A biohazard suit might be a good delivery room choice.

You need to wear comfortable clothes to the scene of the crime. They need to be clothes that you aren't too attached to. Don't wear your old high-school football jersey. You may want to toss all of these clothes afterwards. The delivery room is a very messy place. If you look down, you will see a drain in the floor; it is there for a reason.

*The **number one draft pick** is your little star.*

Better than old clothes would be a full hazmat suit, complete with face shield and oxygen supply. Let's face it; the delivery room is a messy and smelly place. I imagine after the room is empty a nuclear waste disposal team comes in to clean up—three people in full suits manning a fire hose as they wash down the walls, floors, and ceiling to ready the room for the next youngster. Keep the hazmat suit for when your star starts solid foods; you will need it.

LIVE ACTION SHOTS

Guys have seen many births on television and in the movies, but it ain't the same in real life (unless you watch the Discovery Channel). On television they always hand a perfectly clean baby, a perfect little miniature adult, to the mom as the supportive dad leans on the bed. But reality is different. Your baby is going to be covered in all manner of gunk.

If your baby comes out through the birth canal, your baby will not look like a mini adult. It will look like a wrinkled old man who spent too long in the pool at his condo in Florida. And your little star will be covered with a substance that looks like petroleum jelly. Oh, and the head will be funny looking too.

Touchdown

 Your star will look like the world's prettiest raisin when you first see her.

All of these scenarios are natural. First, babies are waterlogged; they just spent nine months in the pool. Actually, the womb is more like scuba diving. Once you see your number one draft pick, a few wrinkles aren't going to matter. They go away fairly quick.

Second, the petroleum jelly is a natural protective covering that will be washed off in the nursery. This gunk is a layer of protection while your little star is swimming like a dolphin. And she will be bluish in color, with puffy eyes. But she will still be beautiful to you.

Third, the bones in the skull are flexible so the head can fit through the birth canal. The bones of the skull don't fuse and become completely solid until after you drop them once. Just kidding. It will happen in about six months (and don't ever drop your kid). A friend told me that his wife gave birth to a Tylenol pill. The head will gradually become round again.

If you have a C-section, the baby's head will probably be round and look closer to normal. The head won't have to be squashed to go through the birth canal. Depending on how far Cletus had dropped, there might be some deformation though. But it still won't be Tylenol shaped. Your star will still be coated with motor oil.

Once the youngster is out, she will still be attached by an extension cord. Okay, it's an umbilical cord and has been her lifeline for the last nine months. The cord is long enough for the baby to be set on mom's chest before cutting. You have the option of cutting the cord. The nurses clamp it off and you snip. But it will be tougher to cut than you think.

Fumble *You have the option of cutting the umbilical cord, but they won't let you bring any power tools.*

You may be given the opportunity to catch the baby as it enters the world. You will be given instructions on what to do. Now is not the time to practice one-handed snags or do any touchdown celebrations once your star is in your hands.

The sound of a crying baby will announce to all in the room that the baby is now in charge. I think the baby is crying because life just got worse. Your baby has been living the high life for nine months. Now he has to breath, eat, cry, and try to make his parents look like idiots. More on how your kid makes you look like an idiot later.

TAKING YOUR DRAFT PICK ON THE ROAD

The nurse sucks mucus out of your little star's nose and mouth with a teardrop-shaped suction device. They don't spank babies to get them breathing anymore. Nurses will take your baby away and place her under a heat light while an expert wrestles with your baby. They are giving your baby her first test, the APGAR test. And I thought my first test was spelling in the first grade.

 The baby's first test comes only minutes into the world.
Fumble

The APGAR test is a general test that describes how well your baby is functioning. Appearance, pulse, grimace, activity, and respiration are the items that are checked. They are looking for a good color, a strong pulse, reaction to pain, good activity, and crying. If the score is too low, they will whisk the baby off to a mini incubator and provide whatever support the baby may need. If you have a C-section, they may take the baby away while they sew mom up.

If you had a vaginal delivery, they might leave the baby to snuggle on the mom's chest. They also might suggest that your baby try breast-feeding right away. Don't worry if your baby won't eat right away. Eating is a new skill for the baby.

Also new for the baby will be the sight of you and mom. She already knows your voices, but your faces will be new.

You and mom might look slightly bedraggled from lack of sleep and intense effort, but you will look beautiful to her, I think. She will open her eyes, look at you, and then close them again.

Baby vision is very crude at first but will develop over the next six months. Your draft pick will only be able to focus about a foot away; everything else will be blurry. This is the perfect distance for breast-feeding, so your star will have plenty of eye contact with the head coach. Babies like to look at objects with a lot of contrast; black and white things look best to her. They also can't see colors early on. Her vision will improve and by three months she will see pretty well. Depth perception is one of the last things to develop, so it is a good thing that they don't crawl yet.

If you have a boy, a decision will have to be made about circumcision. Talk to your pediatrician and obstetrician about the pros and cons. If you decide to do it, do it right away. Most guys don't want that part of their anatomy clipped later.

 *If you have a boy, a decision will have to be made about* **clipping**.

You are now the proud QB dad for your wonderful little star. Look into those little eyes and realize that you will never be the same; you will always be her QB dad. Cherish the moments and savor the memories. Now that she is here, you only have a few preseason activities left. After you leave the hospital, the regular season awaits.

THE COIN FLIP

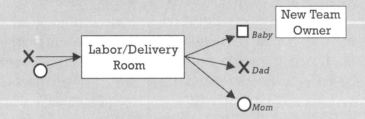

Try not to panic at the hospital.

Ignore any threats she makes during contractions.

Trust the doctors, but feel free to ask questions.

Delivery rooms are messy places.

Prepare yourself for the fact that newborns look funny.

You might be able to catch your baby as she comes out.

You can also cut the cord if you want.

Accept all the congratulations; you are a QB dad now.

STADIUM SEATS ARE NOT COMFORTABLE

Once you are in the room with only the three of you it will sink in. You have a beautiful new star and it came complete with no instruction manual. Funny thing, you buy a toaster and get a twelve-page instruction manual, but with a baby you get stopped on fourth down. Luckily you have this book.

How long you stay in the hospital will depend on what route you took. At a birth center, you may be home in twenty-four hours. At a hospital it is often at least two days. For a C-section, it will probably be three days. Don't rush home. You are surrounded by experts who are incredibly kind and caring.

 A labor and delivery room that is stocked with all the amenities will act as your own **luxury skybox.**

Hospitals have several ways of taking care of births now. They have become more user-friendly since you and I were delivered. Many have a single room for labor, delivery, and your hospital stay. These rooms are outfitted like luxury sky-boxes with all the amenities. Our room had wood furniture, a fridge, fold-out sleeping chair, and a television with a remote. That will allow us to catch up on *SportsCenter* after the baby is here. For god's sake, turn off the television during the delivery. Anyway, they run *SportsCenter* repeats over and over in the morning.

If you have other bigger stars on the team, they may also be allowed to stay with you. Of course, they could also stay with Grammy. Introduce the new star to the veteran stars early. There might be some jealousy, but they will get over it (in about twenty years).

Some hospitals still have a labor/delivery room and a different room for your stay. The room will still be outfitted comfortably and will provide a place for you to stay with your head coach.

One choice you will have is rooming in with the baby. This means that the baby will stay in the room with you, other than periodic escapes to the nursery for the pediatrician to look her over. Rooming in is kind of neat, but I wouldn't recommend it for the first night. That first night you both need rest. The head coach either had major surgery or intense labor, and you probably haven't slept much. Besides, you will have enough sleepless nights in the first three months. A nurse will bring your star in when it's feeding time.

 *Don't start baby races in the hallways with the other new*
Fumble *dads.*

The baby will have this wonderful little plastic crib complete with a nameplate and tons of blankets. The best part is that the crib is on wheels. I wanted to start my own baby race in the hallways with the other new dads, but I was overruled by the head coach. I was going to call it the Diaper Derby. Could've taken bets and made a little money. Darn.

A Word about Hospital Beds

The head coach will be propped up on a bed that befits a queen. It has controls to raise and lower all parts. It also has a remote control and built-in television speakers. Your head coach will be living the life of luxury with three hundred thread-count sheets. I was secretly jealous of the bed.

You are not as important as the head coach to the nurses and staff. They will ask her all sorts of question and cater to her every whim. They will bring her more pillows, pain medication, hot food, and pretty much anything she asks for. You, on the other hand, have to fend for yourself. Good luck.

Touchdown

 As the staff comes in to check on the head coach, you realize that you are a bit player in the hospital's eyes.

You will be provided with a fold-out chair that doubles as a bed. These beds are actually medieval torture devices that will be covered with a burlap rag for a sheet. After a few nights sleeping on this bed, you will long for sleeping anywhere else. At least now you might sympathize with the prisoners on Alcatraz. Don't worry; you'll get plenty of sleep once you are back safely in your own locker room.

A WORD ABOUT HOSPITAL FOOD

Every four to five hours someone will show up with hot food for your wife. Okay, it is still hospital food, but it is warm. A few of the meals will even look good. Be prepared: Virtually every tray of hospital food comes with Jello. I was under the impression only old people and kids eat Jello. But in the hospital everybody gets it.

You are on your own for food for the duration of your stay. While your wife gets a tray and linen napkins, you will probably be sitting at the world's smallest table eating an egg salad sandwich from a vending machine. I think my egg salad was left over from the Clinton administration.

Hospital vending machines are like the White House: They get filled with new selections every four years.
Fumble

If you had the foresight to follow my advice from earlier, you will have plenty of granola bars, chips, and snacks for the midnight munchies. That at least ensures that you get something edible during your stay. Actually, hospital cafeterias have a much wider and healthier selection than in bygone days. During certain hours they have salad bars and edible hot food. An ice-cream bar as a surprise from the cafeteria can also be a big hit with the head coach.

More important than your own hunger is keeping the head coach well fed and as happy as possible. Your head coach might be back on a regular diet and able to eat anything as soon as several hours after delivering. If you really want to earn points with the coach, pull out the phone. Ask your best friend to pick up her favorite food, and tell him to buy extra, because your wife is ravenous. You can help him smuggle it in. You and the friend both look like heroes (and you can eat the leftovers). As the QB dad, it is important to make critical decisions at crunch time.

If you really want to win the MVP trophy, have her favorite restaurant meal brought in. Ask the nurse for a clean plate and serve her like a waiter. She will love the sentiment and you will be a star in her eyes. Make sure it is her favorite restaurant and not yours! She will see that for the ploy it is.

Our hospital provided one fancy sit-down dinner before we left. They whisked the baby off to the nursery and brought in a gourmet spread. Well, at least as gourmet as hospitals get. If you are lucky enough to get such treatment, enjoy this meal. It may be one of the last meals that you can sit through without worrying about your little superstar.

Touchdown

Calling your best friend and asking him to pick up the head coach's favorite food is a great way to score big points.

After a few days at the hospital, you are ready to take the little star to her new home field. The hospital stay has given you many fond laughs, but now it's time to get serious. Taking the baby home starts the regular season.

STADIUM SEATS ARE NOT THAT COMFORTABLE

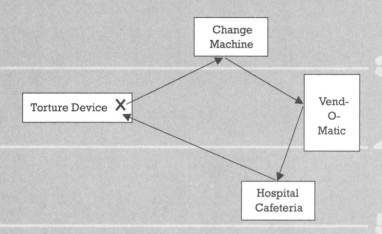

Change Machine

Torture Device ✗

Vend-O-Matic

Hospital Cafeteria

New labor/delivery rooms are actually inviting.

Older children can probably stay in the room with you.

You might want to use the nursery for your baby the first night.

No crib races with the other QB dads.

Your bed will be uncomfortable and tiny.

Find out when the cafeteria serves hot food.

Avoid six-year-old sandwiches in the vending machines.

Part 2

GAME DAY

CHEERING FOR THE
8. HOME TEAM

After a few sleepless nights, you are now ready to head home to your own private locker room. Away games are over for a while. The new family is about to leave the hospital. Leaving the hospital means giving up your security blanket. You are leaving the comfort of twenty-four-hour nursing care, hospital cafeteria food (at least you didn't have to cook it), and qualified baby professionals. The regular season starts as soon as you strap your first-round draft pick into the car. OTAs, training camp, and preseason are over. The regular season awaits.

Leaving the hospital is very similar to player introductions at the Super Bowl. It is a great photo op and only the serious fans are there. You will probably have a few family members and some hospital staff to see you off. The outfit that your star wears home will be picked by your head coach, and you probably won't have any say in the matter. The outfit was probably picked out months before. Take photos and bask in the moment. You could even try hiring the local high-school marching band to send you off. The first car ride is a momentous occasion and the beginning of your life with your new team. Install the car seat ahead of time and have a professional check it for a correct fit. Your pediatrician's office, many police departments, or your local kids' superstore all have trained car seat safety inspectors. It is estimated that up to 85 percent of all car seats are installed incorrectly. Having an expert check your work is only prudent. Besides, this may be the first task as a father that you have done all by yourself without the head coach supervising. You want to do it right.

As you step into your own private locker room, realize your life is going to be different now. Different isn't always bad though. You and your partner now have complete control of a little human life. The child can be molded into an exact duplicate of you, or possibly even better.

EXTRA HELP FOR THE TEAM

The regular season takes a serious game plan. You probably have figured out by now that as the quarterback you always defer to the head coach. She probably has ultimate veto power on most kid-rearing issues. The first few days are also a great chance to bring in some baby experts to help. Think of them as special consultants brought in to help your team run more smoothly, kind of like an assistant to the GM.

 Sitting in the den while your house guests cook is not a smart idea.

Fumble

The first few weeks home is a great time for parents and in-laws to stay for extended periods. If you have parents in the house during this time, your life will become easier. They will probably take care of many meals. Try to be helpful as they cook. This is a great time for a television in the kitchen. You can watch ESPN while being supportive.

You might want to establish rules with a war room sit-down (like NFL coaches deciding who to draft) before they stay. This may be delicate or impossible depending on your relationship with your parents or your head coach's parents. Most of the experts are going to give advice anyway, so setting ground rules ahead of time may be prudent. You can choose to ignore any advice that you don't feel comfortable with. Also important to understand is that many things with raising a baby have changed since they raised kids. Ultimately, the little linebacker is yours.

Touchdown

Only trust experts who have already raised one or more children.

Think of grandparents as assistant coaches. They will be a great help and take care of many small tasks. As said before, it might be a time to grow closer to your parents or the head coach's parents. Remember, they have raised kids already and have some experience. But the rules have changed since they raised kids. Solid food starts later and babies sleep on their backs are just two of the new rules. Just establish ground rules first and it will be surprisingly smooth. The extra help is needed and appreciated.

I get along great with my in-laws, but that is not the case for many QB dads. If your teammate's mother takes over the house for a few weeks, just deal with it. Unless the head coach stands up to her, you have zero chance. Your head coach's mother probably means well and wants to make her daughter's life easier. And if the head coach's life is easier, yours will be too. Kill her with kindness as you thank her for meals, cleaning, laundry, and any other tasks she does.

 Illegal procedure *is when your parents hand a stinky baby back to you to change instead of them doing it. Throw the flag.*

Veteran grandparents will be smart enough to leave many tasks for you. The number one task left to you will be diaper changing. New grandparents may long for the nostalgia of changing diapers; veterans will not.

The other school of thought is that the QB dad and head coach should be the only two in the house to help bond with the baby. You will have plenty of time to bond with your superstar in the first year. If you want extra help, don't be afraid to ask. Ultimately, the head coach will probably have the final say in this debate.

 If your parents or in-laws actually enjoy diaper changing, build an in-law suite and let them move in permanently.

Whether you have the house for just your team or if you have assistant coaches on hand, the first few months are trying. Your number one draft pick is going to need the world to revolve around her. She will eventually become more responsive to you and the silly faces that you make. Listen, be supportive, and embrace your growing role on the team.

Friends and coworkers want to feel like they have helped the new star in some small way. When they ask if you need anything, hand them the grocery list. Just kidding, but they truly want to help. They will offer food, help running errands, free baby-sitting, and if they have kids, tons of free advice on baby rearing. If they don't have kids, they will probably offer even more free advice on kid rearing. Funny thing is free advice may not always be free.

Most friends are going to want to come and see the baby in the first few days home. Check with the head coach and then invite them over. Tell them on the phone ahead of time that the visit will have to be short. This will be fine for all of your friends except one. All new parents have one friend that comes over and wants to overstay his welcome. We will call this friend the Pest. He or she may mean well, but the name still fits.

N F L **Prevent defense** *is using the baby to get out of doing something in a polite manner.*

Getting the Pest to leave is difficult. Yawning, leaving the room, and playing Yanni on the stereo won't cause him to decide to leave on his own. Changing into your sleep clothes might work but is still doubtful. If you look like a real NFL QB, this tactic will not work on women. It will encourage them to stay longer. Just politely say "I think the baby has had enough excitement for the day" as you head toward the door. This will probably be your first time using the baby to extricate yourself from an awkward situation, but it won't be the last. Think of a baby as your own prevent defense.

EARLY BABY TIPS

As wonderful as your new prospect is, you need to learn a few facts. First fact: Scientists say that newborns don't smile (in a social sense) for six weeks or so. Friends, parents, and even your pediatrician are going to say "it's just gas" when your newborn smiles. Take heart though, babies smile when they are content. Going to sleep, a gas bubble, and urinating can all bring out a glimpse of the smiles to come. Anybody that has ever drunk too much beer at a ballgame understands smiling while you urinate.

Second fact: Newborns cry. You have to learn to be able to listen to it. Of course, you need to respond to her. Newborns always cry for some reason: hunger, gas, loneliness, wetness, or any reason for discomfort. Crying is the only way that your little star has to communicate. You are not going to spoil the child by responding, even though this is a common fear. Experts say that the reverse is actually true. You will raise a more well-adjusted baby because she will learn to trust that you will make it better. Many of these early cries will be tearless. Crying with tears comes later, like when you won't let her date until she's twenty.

Third fact: Newborns like noise. They just left a place that was noisier than Colts Stadium on game day: the womb. White noise generators, shushing in their ear, playing the radio, and even really bad singing can quiet them down.

Fourth fact: Newborns like to be swaddled. This is a trick that you must learn as a dad. Ask one of the nurses at the hospital to teach you before you leave—they are more than willing to show you. Swaddling was the easiest way to get my daughter to sleep. It should always be part of your baby two-minute drill.

GETTING USED TO YOUR NEW DUTIES

You are going to meet the new boss of the house: your star. The entire world revolves around her eating, elimination (clinical term for poop), and sleeping patterns. An uninterrupted eight hours of sleep is a distant memory. Babies need to eat every three hours or so because their stomach is smaller than your fist. Some experts even say to wake the kid up every three hours to eat. I have one thing to say to those experts: *Are you crazy?* Ask your pediatrician if it's OK to let her sleep if she's sleeping. If your head coach is breast-feeding, you're most likely exempt from feeding the star. However, there are quite a few duties that you can—and should—help out with.

Diaper Changing

Diaper changing the first few days is a treat. Your baby will at first secrete some type of sludge that looks like it came out of the transmission of a 1974 Volvo. Don't worry; this is completely normal. The first bowel movements (a fancy term for poop) will be a substance called meconium that looks like dark greenish-black tar. This is good because it means your baby's intestines are wide open.

N F L **Wide open** *used to mean a receiver streaking down the sideline; now it means the poop is flowing.*

Over the next few months, you will see almost every color imaginable contained in her diaper. My wife actually changed a diaper full of sea foam green poop one time. If your star is breast-fed, the surprising part is that the odor is not all that offensive. Formula-fed babies tend to smell the place up a little more. At about six months of age, babies start solid food, then watch out. Your eyes will water as you pull the diaper off. Break out the hazmat suit you used in the delivery room. Diaper changing will evolve as the kid gets more mobile, but more on that later.

Clean the Uniforms and Field

As the QB, you will do the laundry by yourself the first few weeks home. After all, you are a caring and sensitive guy. Just like in the NFL, the head coach needs to feel needed. You want to share this activity once the head coach is up and about.

Touchdown

Try to do a good job with laundry, but not a great job (if you know what I mean).

Sending out your laundry may also work, but it can get expensive. The look and feel of a freshly pressed dress shirt is guaranteed to make you look more impressive. And the Laundromat actually knows how to fold fitted bed sheets. It must be a secret they learn in dry cleaners school. When I fold a fitted sheet, it looks like I wadded it up.

Laundry is not something most guys enjoy, but we learn how to do it. Guys also don't wash clothes unless they are actually dirty. Guys understand the sniff test: If it smells clean, it is clean. Many of us have used this for years. We know how to go two weeks without doing laundry, if needed. We learned this years ago; many guys only did laundry once a semester in college. On the other hand, the head coach will want to wash everything that touches your star. She also wants to wash everything that touches you or her. With a baby, your number of laundry loads will at least triple. The head coach will also expect you to separate clothes based on color. Do the best you can. After all, you are a helpful guy. And with a baby around, you really have to worry about germs. So the head coach is right; clean clothes are probably important.

Your household only grew by one person, but your laundry will triple. You will probably go through two outfits for every eight hours you spend with her. Your star will go through at least two and probably three outfits a day. The head coach may also like to change her just to use all of the many clothes you will receive.

I am not sure baby's clothes ever wear out. Never turn down hand-me-down clothes if offered. Babies usually outgrow clothes and shoes long before they wear out. When your star outgrows them, hand them down to friends and earn good karma. Don't hand down ugly clothes unless you do it as a practical joke. If you have a particularly hideous outfit, hand it down to one of your good friends. Every time you see your friend, ask him why his baby isn't wearing the outfit you handed down. Feign anger and disgust at his lack of consideration.

You might want to consider hiring a maid until the kid reaches one year. Heck, if you can afford it, hire a maid until your kid reaches thirty. Hopefully by thirty your kid has moved out. Maids do a great job and will most likely clean better than you. Housecleaning when you are sleep deprived is not easy. Another option is to find someone to come in and clean weekly or biweekly.

Touchdown

If you can afford it, hire a maid until your kid reaches one year old.

The prevailing thought is that most guys are slobs, but this is not always the case. Guys are selectively slobby. Me personally, slobby is okay in the bedroom and gameroom but not okay in the kitchen and bathroom. You need to learn to be comfortable in your level of slobbiness.

With your new star in the house, there will be piles of baby-related stuff around—unopened shower gifts to return, newly folded baby clothes, a two-feet-high stack of baby washcloths and diapers. A must is a diaper pail that is designed to hermetically seal diapers into plastic cocoons. You have to make sure the house is not growing bacteria. The superstar has a young immune system, so the house needs to be clean.

NEEDS OF THE HEAD COACH

During these first few days home, treat your partner like a queen. She has just endured what no man will ever endure. The baby got out of her body in one of two ways: She had major surgery or pushed a football through a garden hose.

A NEWBORN'S FIRST FEW DAYS AT HOME

**Crib-Diaper-Bottle/Breast-Pace-Crib.
Repeat every 2 to 3 hours.**

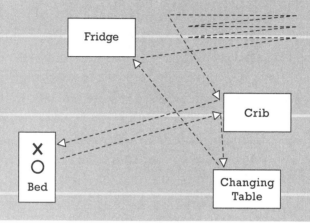

Allow the experts to help.

Talking about baby poop will become standard.

Newborns don't smile in a traditional sense.

Newborns cry.

Newborns like noise.

Newborns love to be swaddled.

Newborns eat every three hours.

Change as many early diapers as possible.

Let's be real; if it was up to guys to have the babies, most of us wouldn't be here. Women supposedly create some hormone that makes them actually forget the pain. I broke an arm, and let me tell you, I still remember the pain.

Spend the first few days home bonding with your wife and the baby. Take a "babymoon" from work, if possible. It won't be as much fun as the honeymoon, but it will help your team function better. Stop by work only to deliver candy bars, cigars, and show pictures of your new all-star to your coworkers. This is a great time to line up free tickets to future games. A few more sleepless nights and you are officially in the dad fraternity.

Your life at home will be an adjustment, but it's worth it. You will get to see your superstar grow and change immensely over the first year. The regular season is in full gear now.

DEALING WITH SLEEP DEPRIVATION

Both of you are going to have to deal with sleep deprivation for the first few months. As your star's sleep patterns stabilize, your own sleep patterns will stabilize. Sleep deprivation is like camping out all night for tickets to a big game. You look back later and wonder how you did it. You can survive a little lost sleep in the long run. Baby-sitting and sharing nighttime duties will help lead to a better team.

Dealing with a newborn takes patience. A newborn will disrupt your schedule and you will be at her mercy. But your little linebacker will reward you with many smiles and laughter over the coming years.

How do you (and the head coach) deal with sleep deprivation? Gone are the nights of eight hours of glorious shuteye. If you're lucky, you still get eight hours of sleep—over the course of two or three days. And the sleep will come in restless four-hour blocks with an occasional nap. Power naps are lifesavers, unless they are done during a meeting with the boss. In the first few months, the boss might even understand. You will get more sleep than the head coach if she breast-feeds. Breast-feeding is so beneficial to the child, and the fact that it benefits you will be our secret.

A baby's sleep patterns will get better after the first four or five months. A newborn star will sleep up to sixteen to eighteen hours a day. But newborns very seldom sleep longer than three hours straight. The phrase "sleeping like a baby" is not about newborns. They sleep three hours at a time and wake up crying. Try to sleep when your newborn is out. You will wake up when he does, but the head coach will already be awake. Head coaches are more tuned in to the little star than you are. The mommy gene will cause her to wake up instantly. I think my head coach would even wake up before my little star most of the time.

Sleep Patterns

Babies appear to have two sleep modes. The first is a light sleep in which they resemble a blind salamander. They squirm and look as if they are dreaming (perhaps dreaming of milk-laden breasts and ceiling fans?). The other sleep is more like a coma. An atomic explosion wouldn't wake them up from this sleep. The limp arm test will determine if they have reached this stage of nirvana. Lift the arm and drop it. If it thuds back to her side, you can lay her down anywhere and she will slumber away.

Sleep patterns will vary from one child to another but by six months are usually stable. At this time, they will sleep from approximately nine at night until an early feeding at five or so. During this period, they usually settle into two (or more) daytime naps. All kids are different though. If possible, you might try to nap with them at least once during the day. By the end of the first year, almost all kids will sleep through the entire night. Two naps per day will continue into the next year.

Touchdown

 A baby's sleep patterns will stabilize after four to six months.

Bassinets and cribs will only be separated by an electronic umbilical cord called a monitor. How did our parents ever raise us without a monitor? The monitor is a great convenience and gives us some freedom to roam the house. You can travel several rooms away and still keep an ear out for signals from your little star. Monitors have supersensitive microphones that will pick up all manner of tiny noises. The slightest noise will cause you and the head coach to spring into action.

Keeping the baby up late may depend on your schedule, not the baby's. A baby doesn't have to get up early for school yet. My head coach wouldn't get home some nights until seven, so we allowed our star to stay up past nine. Both parents need time with the little one. If she went to bed at eight, my head coach would have hardly seen her. Find a bedtime that works for your team. There is no "one-size-fits-all" solution for baby's sleep.

Touchdown

The bed time of a baby can be adjusted slightly for your schedule.

Take turns getting the baby at night if she is formula fed. This is a great time to bond with the baby. Take an active role in nighttime feedings. For breast-feeding, you can be the deliveryman. If the baby is doing formula, just alternate turns, if the head coach lets you. Offer to get the star, even if she says no.

THE BABY SITTER

Taking a couple's timeout is great for the relationship with the head coach. This means that you will have to find a suitable baby sitter that you trust with your little bundle of joy. This may not be as easy as it seems. A good baby sitter is like a stud running back on your fantasy football team: a reliable player who is coveted by all of your friends. If you find a great baby sitter, tell no one!

*Using babysitters for a **timeout** is an effective strategy for your team.*

Try family first, if that is an option. Mom, the senior QB dad, and your partner's parents may be the first choices if they live close. They are trustworthy and probably already know your baby ground rules. As an added bonus, you probably don't have to pay them. If you leave them at their house, make sure they have a babyproofed area in which to cheer on your star. The grandparents may also be the perfect choice to watch her as you escape for a weekend away. Take your head coach away for a birthday or anniversary weekend instead of exchanging gifts. You'll spend a fair amount of time discussing the little one, but there will still be romance. It is also great bonding time for the grandparents.

Touchdown

 Family members can make trusted and cheap baby sitters.

Aunts and uncles are also great choices for low-cost baby-sitting. And if you have nieces or nephews that she can play with, you can get an added benefit of social skills for the baby. Your little star could be the hit of the evening and a treat for the cousins. Of course, you may have to trade off with them and watch the nieces or nephews.

Neighbors may be another option for baby-sitting. They get to bond with the newest addition to the block. Older neighbors that would like grandkids can have a trial run. Grandparents whose own grandkids don't live close are especially eager fans. Your star may be the perfect way to bring the neighborhood together. These are the same neighbors that will form a neighborhood watch in a few years anyway. The neighborhood watch is that collection of neighborhood spies that you hated as a teenager. They are grownup versions of the schoolyard tattletale. They told every time you had a party or had friends over. As a parent, you may grow to love this group of neighbors.

A neighborhood teenager is often the baby sitter elect. Trustworthiness is the number one concern with teens. It helps if you know the parents. Set up a few ground rules like no boys, no long phone calls, a baby bedtime, and no boys. Remember back to when you were a sixteen-year-old boy and what you would have done to get alone with a good looking teenage baby sitter.

Fumble *Never tell friends if you find a great baby sitter; they will drive up the price when they try to steal them.*

So you've found a good baby sitter and you are off. What to do on a date? It may have been a while since you actually went on a date with the head coach. Keep the first few trips short, maybe a nice dinner. Once you trust your little one and the baby sitter, you can try games, movies, theater, and anything that you enjoy. Hold hands, smooch, and keep the head coach from calling home every three minutes. Try to keep baby talk to a minimum.

N F L *QB dads are usually looking for ways to increase* **playing time** *with the head coach.*

Romance between the parents is important for the health of your relationship. A healthy relationship will lead to healthier children. Think of the two of you getting away as extra time spent after a football practice. Just you and the head coach working on future game plans. And this may lead to increased playing time.

STAYING HEALTHY

One of the upsides of these first few days is you will also be able to take charge of the house—for a short period of time anyway. Think of this time as calling audibles at the line of scrimmage. You will be making many snap decisions. One of your major responsibilities is to make sure that the head coach is eating a well-balanced diet. This is especially important if she is breast-feeding. She will be taking a multivitamin, but she still needs a well-balanced diet. You might have to learn how to clean, cook, and eat veggies. Of course, frozen veggies are already cleaned and just as healthy.

If you know the difference between imported spices and the Spice Girls, you can ignore the next few paragraphs. Living off takeout and mac n' cheese probably worked in the early years, but now you have to be more sophisticated. And I am not talking about the deluxe mac n' cheese. Takeout might still work for one meal a day, but the costs will quickly add up.

Fumble *If your idea of a well-balanced meal is a balance of nachos, cheeseburgers, and ice cream, you will have to change once you have a kid.*

My idea of a well-balanced meal was a balance of nachos, cheeseburgers, and ice cream. If you're like me, that will have to change once you have a kid. Your child is going to watch what you eat and mimic you. With childhood obesity reaching epidemic proportions, it is vital that your kid learns good eating habits early in life. You will also feel better yourself by eating better.

Free Food

One advantage of friends coming over is that they will bring you more stuff. Even if they already bought you a shower gift, they feel like they can't arrive at your house empty-handed. Here is a great tactic to steer their impulses. When they call and ask to come over, just drop the line, "I was just getting ready to make some ramen noodles for dinner." This almost always results in my favorite thing: free food. Even bad free food is still free (and you didn't have to cook it).

Comfort foods are important for your first few days home. I live in the South and Southerners love nothing more than a good casserole. Southerners will turn anything into a casserole—green beans, broccoli, potatoes, all meats, and even Jello. Of course, by the time they are done with it, it only sounds healthy. Eating a good casserole could double your cholesterol.

When it comes to pregnancy food, everyone turns Southern. Friends will bring over complete casseroles that are already frozen, ready to cook on a moment's notice. The directions will be taped to the top. These casseroles could actually serve as a meal. Broccoli casserole goes perfect with that guy staple, the hot dog. Every guy knows how to cook hot dogs perfectly: on the grill until the skin just begins to puff up. If your friends bring over Jello salad or any other type of congealed salad, politely thank them. After they leave, head directly to the garbage disposal, do not pass go, do not collect two hundred dollars.

Takeout is even better because it usually comes with its own plate. You get the grub with no dishes to do. That is my idea of the perfect meal: free food and no clean up.

Touchdown

If you live in an urban setting, people will probably bring takeout.

Another free food strategy is the "My wife (or girlfriend) just loves (insert head coach's favorite food)" strategy. When friends call, ask them to stop by your favorite bakery and pick up a particular treat. Say, "My wife (or girlfriend) just loves the (insert favorite pastry and bakery here). Could you pick up a few on the way?" Nobody turns down new moms, or in this case a new dad. Offer to pay them back when they arrive; they will turn down your invitation. You make points with the head coach and you get free pastries. This strategy can be adapted for Chinese food, pizza, and many other wants. You could even use a city map with colored pins highlighting choices for easy reference when the phone rings.

Your little star will settle into a routine during the first few months. Laundry duty, cleaning, and baby sitters all help the team function better. Keeping all the team members well fed and happy is a vital task for the QB dad. Your role in the household has grown and you will be rewarded for that, someday.

CALLING A TIMEOUT

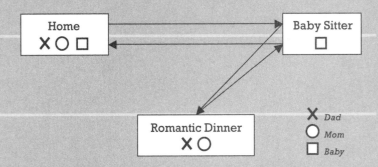

Home
✗ ◯ ☐

Baby Sitter
☐

Romantic Dinner
✗ ◯

✗ Dad
◯ Mom
☐ Baby

EXTRA POINTS

Newborns sleep up to eighteen hours a day.

Encourage the head coach to breast-feed.

Babies have two levels of sleep.

Sleep patterns usually stabilize by four to six months.

Take a couple's timeout and go on dates to keep the romance alive.

Try family first for baby-sitting, if they live close.

If you find a good baby sitter, tell no one!

Friends will steal baby sitters.

HOT DOGS AND NACHOS FOR
9. YOUR LITTLE STAR

Feeding your little star starts out pretty easy but gets progressively more complicated. Restaurant trips and solid food are just a few of the things that you will learn to look at differently. Luckily, it is a fairly slow buildup before the real difficult choices have to be made.

For the first four to six months, your star's diet will consist of formula or breast milk—nothing else. Your mother-in-law may say to add some rice, but most experts will warn you otherwise. I am not a nutritionist, just a dad, so ask your pediatrician. The guidelines I give are what worked for us.

BREAST-FEEDING

The decision to breast-feed or to use formula has already been made and it was probably made for you. Breast-feeding is the hands-down winner for your baby's health and well-being. Most experts will tell you to breast-feed, if you can. Formula wins on the ease-of-use front, but it can be expensive, and experts report that breast milk is better for the baby overall. Of course, if the head coach breast-feeds, you have it a lot easier. You can volunteer to help, but darn, you just can't produce any milk.

Encourage your wife to breast-feed if she is physically able and feels comfortable doing so. It is good for the baby in many ways. And at 3 AM you can roll over (after you bring the baby to your wife) since you don't have working breasts. Never, under any circumstances, tell her that breast-feeding is easier for you. Be helpful and pitch in to do other duties instead. Breast-feeding is a perfect place to lend your expertise. One of the most common ways to hold a breast-feeding baby is called the "football hold." She tucks the little one under her arm like a pigskin and cradles the head just like you cradle the tip of the ball. To prevent fumbles, keep the ball (baby) high and tight as she eats away. She does have the advantage of doing this without wild-eyed linebackers chasing her.

Fumble *They actually make a bladder and tube contraption so you can breast-feed. Do not let your wife know this.*

If your wife pumps breast milk, you can use a bottle and feed it to the little one. Feeding is a time to bond with the baby, and try to do it occasionally with a bottle (if the head coach will let you). Some women are very possessive about feedings; some will let anybody feed the little star.

If your wife uses a breast milk pump, do yourself a big favor and *never* watch her do it. The image will be seared into your retina forever. That mechanical device mauling at the head coach's breasts will be a hindrance to your future love-making. You will finally realize once and for all what breasts are actually for. And aren't you the person who is supposed to maul her breasts?

Never watch the head coach use a breast pump.
Fumble

Formula is a good backup plan even if you breast-feed. Measure out the amount needed into a dry bottle. Keep it with you when you're on the go without the boss. Just add water according to the formula directions when the star wants it and you are the hero. They also make a myriad of plastic containers to premeasure and carry formula.

Be prepared: Women will want to marry you when they see you, a solo dad, feeding a baby. If you are married (or in a serious relationship), fight them off. If you are a single QB dad, enjoy.

EARLY SOLIDS

You will probably start the baby off on solid food with cereal. It is not a manly cereal like Captain Crunch or Wheaties but a wimpy-looking, watered-down, oatmeal-looking concoction. This goop will most likely be the first new taste of the baby's life. Don't tell your head coach that the baby has already tasted things you let her suck off your finger. That will be a secret between you and the baby. This is not recommended, but many dads have given their star a little taste of something along the way when the head coach wasn't looking. But me, of course, I never let my star have anything early. No, I didn't.

The next food your baby will try will most likely be jarred solid baby food (usually fruits or vegetables). Solid food for babies is a misnomer. Baby food is not solid and it doesn't even look like food. I think baby food companies just open cans of vegetables and turn on a blender. A single can will fill six baby food jars and the baby food company profits. Or maybe the baby food companies get the scraps that won't fit in the cans at the other factory. Either way, baby food companies are like a Super Bowl champion quarterback—just raking in the cash. Baby food comes in all price ranges, from el cheapo brands all the way up to organic brands. The head coach will give you detailed instructions on which to buy, if she ever lets you buy any.

You can actually make your own baby food, if you have more free time than me. I have a friend who made all of her own ground-up concoctions. She said that way she could control what went into it. My blender only gets used for margaritas, so I don't think it would be safe for making baby food.

 *Ground meat for babies will resemble no meat you have* **Fumble** *ever seen.*

I was okay with all of the ground-up fruit and vegetables, but the meat was another story. The little bottles of meat had a noxious smell that made me gag. Guys like obnoxious smells—when we create them. We don't want a nasty smell out of a jar. Also, what is in those jars in no ways resembles beef or chicken that I have ever seen. I debated turning my star into a vegetarian, at least until she was old enough to feed herself.

The baby food companies also make the packaging look appealing and create exotic combinations. But when you open the container, they still look like runny slop. Of course, the packaging has to look good to sell a tiny jar for that much money. No baby would ever agree to eat it if she knew better. Babies don't, so they eat it anyway. I am not sure if my daughter liked it anyway, since she always spit up half of what she ate.

New Foods

New foods should be introduced one at a time. You should also have your baby try a new food for a few days to test for any food allergies. You probably won't be making the choices, but it will help you understand why the little one eats peas for five straight days. Some foods should be left until after the first birthday and many until after the second birthday. These include peanuts, seafood, honey, and real milk. Of course, consult with your pediatrician on recommendations.

Touchdown

Consult with your pediatrician on recommendations for when to start different foods.

My head coach kept a detailed diary of when we added each new food. After a food is deemed safe, you can keep using it along with another new food. Once apples pass the test, she can have apples the rest of her life. Our star liked and tolerated everything—even the disgusting ground meat that the head coach fed her—but food allergies are getting more and more common in babies, so it's important to keep track of what foods produced a reaction in your star.

GOING OUT TO THE SNACK BAR

Going out to eat with a newborn is actually pretty easy. A newborn will stay in the carrier and sleep most of the time. Even if she wakes up while you're out, she will usually settle down if you give her a bottle or a breast. If you are breast-feeding, select a table that can easily be transformed into a breast supper table. Booths seem to work the best for this. Just drape a cloth over her head and the little star will eat away in privacy.

Touchdown

 Use the first year to scout for restaurants with healthy kids' menus.

Somewhere in the first year the baby will switch to a high chair and restaurants become a little more difficult. Choose restaurants wisely after your newborn starts using the high chair—absolutely no tablecloths. And if there are more than two forks at each setting, forget it as kids will grab anything and everything within their reach. Look for places that cater to kids and are kid friendly. Four-star dining will be best enjoyed with a baby sitter keeping the kid.

In restaurants, position your star so she has maximum vis-ibility. She will be more interested in every other table in the place. She sees you two all the time. Strangers will smile and make faces at her—let them. Heck, encourage them. They are part of the evening's entertainment. And if the baby is happy, everybody's meal is better. Besides, if she causes someone else to smile, it is worth it.

For the entire first year, your little star doesn't need her own meal. You will bring her food with you in the diaper bag (or in the head coach's bra). But it is a good time to scout out restaurants that have good kids' menus. Also check out which restaurants offer Kids Eat Free night and which night of the week it is. You want her to learn healthy eating habits by giving her good choices and modeling good choices. Even fast food places give you pretty good choices today. You will learn to look at restaurants differently once you have a kid.

Dinner and a Show

Late in the first year you will also have to find ways to amuse your star at restaurants while you wait for food. The best choice is to ask the server for a pregame snack. Most restaurants will bring fruit, crackers, and salad stuff early to feed your little ravenous beast. And as a good QB dad, you have loaded the diaper bag with all manner of small snacks that are age appropriate. The baby food companies make several types of snacks that are designed for baby mouths.

This is also a great time to begin a pregame ritual in restaurants. You will have to develop the ability to keep the little one smiling and happy while waiting on food. If other people in the restaurant pitch in, that is wonderful, but sometimes you are on your own. I used Mr. Fingerman, a funny little walking character created with, you guessed it, two fingers.

Mr. Fingerman would strut around the table and hide behind all of the condiments. As soon as my star started to crane her neck to look, he would pop out and surprise her. Mr. Fingerman will stay in my bag of tricks for the next several years.

Mr. Fingerman was just a finger-walking version of that kid classic, peekaboo. Peekaboo is a wonderful way to amuse your star. Other people in the restaurant will also join in and play by looking over table dividers.

Germs and Mess Prevention

You might get a high-chair cover as a baby gift. This is a useful device for high chairs and grocery store carts. My head coach and I unwrapped one together and she oohed and aahed over it. I thought to myself, "no way will I use that without her." I was wrong. High chairs and grocery carts are some of the nastiest things I have ever seen. You probably haven't paid attention to these oversized petri dishes if you don't have a kid, but once you're a QB dad you'll see what I mean. And be aware that your star will want to chew on every available space, so it is best to cover surfaces with something that at least has her own germs on it. These covers are also a benefit when the little one nods off. Our cover came with a matching pillow that was perfect when she went to sleep.

Bibs

Bibs are a must once your little star starts to eat on her own. At home, just dress your star in "redneck formal" (wearing only a diaper) when feeding. Cleanup is easy and you can redress her after lunch or breakfast. But when you are out to eat, naked is just not proper. They make disposable bibs, which are a great convenience. Keep a box in the car. They also make bibs that look like artist smocks and cover everything. I have friends that swear by the smocks. And besides, the little one will be painting every reachable surface anyway. Food painting is just an early form of finger painting. Don't try to stifle that creativity by telling her no. Picasso's mom let him paint with food early and he turned out okay.

NACHOS

Once your star is able to eat solid foods and you've pre-screened the ingredients for allergies and choking hazards, the ultimate baby food is nachos. We are talking about the piled high, loaded nachos from the appetizer menu. Nachos also cover most of the food categories groups in one sitting. And the best fact is that nachos are plenty messy. Kids love messy food. As adults, we try to hit our mouths most of the time when we eat. Kids, on the other hand, share the wealth. If it tastes good, it must also feel good when smeared on her face, hair, arms, legs, and every surface that is near. Most nachos also appear slightly digested already.

Let's examine nachos for health. The base layer is corn tortilla chips and the ground corn used to make the tortilla chips is a grain, so that covers the bottom category of the food pyramid right there. Next is the meat and beans, which are a great source of protein. And we all know that cheese is a healthy dairy product. We have already covered three of the six. Finish it off with lettuce, tomato, and peppers from the vegetable category, and add guacamole with its "good" fat to cover the top of the pyramid. Finish the meal off with fresh fruit and you've just covered the whole pyramid.

 Ultimate nachos cover the major food categories.

Stadium nachos can fill the bill in a pinch if you need healthy baby food. Stadium nachos come with corn chips and a cheese sauce. At least, I think it is a cheese sauce. Sneak over to the condiment table and load it up with lettuce and tomato to make it even healthier. The head coach will be so proud that you fed your star a well-balanced meal on your own. Nachos are also the ultimate sports food, messy and tasty at the same time. Of course, they are more of a QB dad food than a baby food. You probably don't want to feed a six-month-old salsa and chips. But it is never too early to be thinking about good baby nutrition. You will be spending many weekend days cheering with your star in the future and good food is a must.

Over the first year, food will go from the most important thing in a baby's life to just one little thing. The head coach may make all of the important food decisions, but be helpful. Later in life you will decide hot dogs or nachos at the ballgame, so let the head coach enjoy those early decisions.

BURPING

Memo to all QB dads: You will become the burping expert. All dads have the innate ability to get the little one to burp. It

DINING OUT WITH YOUR STAR

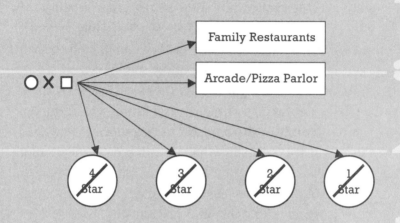

Family Restaurants

Arcade/Pizza Parlor

4 Star

3 Star

2 Star

1 Star

Try to share in the early feedings, even if the head coach breast-feeds.

Never watch your wife use a breast pump.

Solid food for babies is not solid and only slightly resembles food.

You will become the baby burping expert.

Going out to eat with a newborn is fairly easy.

Use early trips to scout out restaurants with healthy kids' menus.

Encourage strangers to help entertain your little star.

Nachos are the ultimate baby food.

might go back to being able to burp on command in middle school. It is just a guy skill.

The first thing to know is to never wear a good shirt when burping. Your star will usually just burp, but sometimes she will projectile vomit white slime all over your shoulder. My star's upchuck always seemed to be a shade of white, even after she started eating all of those exotic combinations of baby food. They have burp cloths, but my star always missed the cloth. Burp towels might work, if they were beach towels.

There are several techniques for burping your little one. The old favorite is the baby on the shoulder. A few dozen pats on the back and she will make you proud. The shoulder routine always worked best for me. You can also support the chest of your star in one hand while she is sitting in your lap. A few pats and the gas bubble is popped.

Be prepared: The head coach and family members will cheer when the baby burps and will be quite proud of her, but when you burp nobody cheers. That just isn't right. Don't we wish the head coach was proud of all of our skills?

HITTING THE
10. SHOWERS

Just like all football players wear a uniform, so do babies. Shoulder pads are required gear for football players; diapers are required gear for babies. The outside jersey may be different, but the base layer is basically the same.

 *The **team uniform** (diaper) is worn by all babies.*

There are two basic types of diapers: cloth and disposable. Let's face it; this choice will most likely be made by the head coach. You will get some input. Unless you have very strong feelings one way or the other, just say "Yes, Dear." Both types have advantages and disadvantages.

CLOTH DIAPERS

Cloth diapers were the hit of the early twentieth century, but like the single wing offense they have all but disappeared. Some people choose to use cloth diapers because they can be cheaper and are better for the environment. They definitely don't fill up landfills the way their disposable cousins do. If you wash them yourself, they are probably cheaper. Babies in cloth diapers are usually potty trained earlier. And old diapers are perfect for polishing your trophies, if they have been washed first.

Fumble *Most QB dads never put a diaper on a doll or longed for the day that we could change a diaper.*

Cloth diapers may actually be more expensive than disposables if you use a service. There are diaper services that will launder and supply you with new diapers. But you still have to do some early dirty work to dispose of the solids (fancy word for crap). They take tons of hot water, bleach, and soap to make them usable again. And cloth diapers smell; they will outwit the best air freshener.

DISPOSABLE DIAPERS

Disposable diapers are the hands-down winners for most new babies. They offer the ease of convenience and disposability. Did I mention they smell less? However, they are expensive. And they fill up landfills at an astonishing rate. Since your baby doesn't feel any wetness with the latest diaper technology, there is usually less diaper rash than with cloth diapers. The baby will go through about 3,000 diapers before she masters the throne, so diapering is a skill that you must learn. And like throwing the ball away to avoid a sack, it is a skill that must be learned.

Be Prepared

Don't let yourself run out of disposable diapers. Buy extras, and lots of them. Diapers are sold with weights shown on the package, and there is some overlap in these weights. You have at least one to two months where two different sizes will fit. A little big and they stay on better, but too big and they leak. Emergencies (when you run out) will take ingenuity, such as crafting a diaper out of two rag towels and duct tape. Just avoid this by buying extras. Buy the large boxes and stock up.

CHANGING A DIAPER 101

Several things are needed to diaper the baby: diapers (duh!), wipes, and diaper cream. You also need a flat, safe spot to do it. It also helps to have a changing pad (with straps) that is designed for this duty. Make sure all of your materials are within arm's reach. Later you can attempt a standing diaper change, but not with newborns.

 A **blitz** is an unexpected movement while the baby is uncovered during a diaper change.

Place the baby on the pad and use the strap. Never leave a baby alone on the pad. Open and slide a new diaper under the old one, in case you get a blitz. With a boy, this means the fountain is on. Boys will cover you, the walls, and everything in the room with wee-wee. A helpful hint is to place a washcloth over the hose for boys as soon as you undo the old diaper.

Using the ankle lift, clean all the offensive areas with wipes. Make sure you clean the genital areas very well and always wipe front to back. Slide out the dirty diaper and wad up the wipes inside the diaper. Make sure the baby is dry before sealing up the new diaper to cut down on diaper rash. Before sealing the diaper, let her air dry for a moment. With boys, be careful of the short pass over the middle. A little diaper rash cream should be used if any areas appear red. Be aware: Women will use diaper cream every time. Guys only use it when needed.

After drying and applying cream, use the old adhesive tabs to seal the diaper into a perfect ball. Then spike the football into the diaper pail. You can also try this option if the head coach is in the room: Throw her a perfect pass with the diaper football.

Diaper Rash

Speaking of the importance of diaper cream, diaper rash is no fun for you or your little star. Changing diapers often and letting your little star air dry will help. Also, use diaper cream when needed. Diaper cream is usually the same white zinc oxide that old people in Florida put on their nose to prevent sunburns. They actually sell a product called Butt Paste, and that may be one of the best product names ever. Butt Paste also comes in fifty-five-gallon drums; you ought to go through one drum a year.

MAKE IT FUN

Diaper changing is a perfect opportunity to amuse your star. Silly poop songs were one of my favorite ways to amuse her. Take almost any song and add the word *poop* into some appropriate place in the song.

For example:

Twinkle, Twinkle, Little Poop,
How I wonder what you ate,
Down below your butt so clean,
Looks a lot like chocolate cream.

Sing these songs loud enough for the head coach to hear. If she is offended that you find poop to be so amazing, she might fire you from that duty. Singing is not recommended when you change the baby in a public restroom unless you are in the bathroom at a football game. Then you can sing the team's fight song with pride. Some fans are very serious, so don't replace any words with *poop*.

Fumble *Singing is not recommended when you change the baby in a public restroom.*

Another way to make changing more fun is to do a play by play. Almost all guys are secretly envious of football commentators, and this is your chance to get into the action. And if imitation is the sincerest form of flattery, Troy Aikman would be proud. I changed well over a hundred diapers while imitating the former Cowboy great.

Diaper changing is another place for competition. Try to shoot for the fastest time. Of course, there will have to be two categories: wet and wild. Lean in and try to get the fastest time. My best times were 8.2 seconds and 49.2 seconds.

Silly faces while changing diapers will also help the process along. Make it a point to make the most disgusting but comical face possible when she pops out a winner. A helpful "oowwhhee" is also a nice addition to the routine. The serious parenting books say you shouldn't make rude comments about something that is natural. The authors of those books probably don't fart either. Most guys I know enjoy a good fart.

You should also celebrate your star's successes. A good movement should be rewarded with applause and shouts. Little movements should get a polite golf clap. And of course once the baby is safe on the floor, the Rocky diaper dance is a nice celebration. Just throw your arms in the air like you just won a world championship.

A diaper blowout is best handled by going straight to the tub. A hand-held spray is perfect for blowing the offensive material off her butt, legs, back, and so on. If you are not able to go to the tub, use wipes and plenty of them. Also, check all of her clothes after a blowout. Chances are you will also need to change her outfit, so be aware when you are on the go. Always pack an extra outfit in the diaper bag, if you pack it.

A belly fart is also required in my household after the baby is rediapered. The PC term is *raspberries*, but *belly fart* is a much better term. Belly farts are just a staple in fatherdom. Your star will eventually expect it and start smiling in anticipation. In the second half of the first year, she will start laughing in anticipation. Baby laughter is the sweetest sound.

Your dad may have never changed a diaper. The times they are a changing. Diaper duty is an expected dad duty today. A friend who shall remain nameless is quite proud that he has never changed a diaper. I feel like he actually missed out on an important step in the life of his little star. Don't pass the baby during diaper time. Use this time to bond with your baby.

SHOWERS AFTER THE GAME

Cleaning the baby is an evolving chore in the first year. Baby baths will go from quick sponge baths to a fun play time (for the baby). This is not always the best chore, but it may bring you many laughs as your star grows.

How to Bathe Your Star

The first baby baths are sponge baths. Your star won't be sweating and food will not be for playing in, at least not yet. For about the first six weeks the baths will be quick, neat, and almost waterless. The head coach also may not trust this chore to you. If she forbids you, put up a good show like you really wanted to do it. As always, follow your pediatrician's advice for when to shift to a tub.

Baby tubs are useful and convenient. They allow you to wash the baby on a counter or any easy place. Many tubs will also convert into a seat for the regular tub once they finish sponge baths. You can also just wash her in the sink. Most families have a sink bath picture in their photo album. Sink baths are also perfect for when you are traveling.

Eventually the baby will outgrow any additional tub seat. By this time your star will have a tub full of bath toys. Ducks, stick-on letters, and boats are a must for the tub. Let her enjoy baths and it will save many fights in the next few years. Always stay right at the tub. Never leave a baby in the tub for even a second without you being there. If the phone rings, let the answering machine pick up. Besides, "I was giving the baby a bath" is a great excuse not to pick up the phone.

Touchdown

Many baby tubs convert into safety seats for the big tub.

How Often to Bathe Your Star

For most babies, baths aren't needed every day. Your star simply won't get into enough of a mess—that is, until he starts eating with his hands. Once he starts eating, cleaning the baby means two words: fire hose. I actually wanted to use the hose outside of the house a few times. The head coach vetoed it.

Once they begin to self-feed, nothing you own will ever be clean again. Food will become a play toy. Babies will experiment with their food and push it into every available nook and cranny. They will put it in their hair, nose, eyes, ears, and anywhere on you if you let them. Baths might become a nighttime ritual then. To avoid drying their skin, you can wash without using soap once you start daily baths. Baths are not hard to do and will give you many enjoyable moments. Babies love splashing in the water. Of course, you will get wet too. For a little one, part of the fun must be splashing the parents.

When you give a bath, make sure that you clean the entire baby. Babies have neck rolls. Neck rolls are those cute little rolls of fat that only look good on babies. They also have leg rolls and arm rolls. Little butterball babies look cute. Make sure that you wash in all of the rolls. Use your fingers to spread them out and wash the inside gently.

Touchdown

Splashing the parents will become a sport for your baby.

If you get bath duty, try this occasionally. Go into the bathroom and close the door. Turn on the water and wipe the baby off. Don't put the baby in the tub at all. Heck, in the old days, almost all people only bathed once a week. And if it was good enough for my great-great-grandfather. . . .

Giving a bath means you will be eventually "Caddyshacked." We're talking number two here. Keep an old cup handy to scoop up the material and keep right on bathing. Repeat after me—scoop, flush, continue. Number one will happen without you even knowing. The head coach will not like this, but guys don't care. We always went in the pool growing up anyway. Just don't let your baby drink the water.

HEAVY CLEANUP PREVENTION

A helpful cleaning hint will be repeated here: Dress your baby in only a diaper while she feeds. You can use a bib if you want, but don't let her wear clothes. At restaurants she has to wear clothes, but at home feed her naked. She will wash off, but some foods clean off easier than others. Most early baby foods just wipe right off. Any form of tomato sauce will require scrubbing to remove the red stain from skin. The orange tomato sauce from Spaghetti-Os will stain everything it touches. I have never seen an orange tomato in my life, but all kid's pasta comes with orange tomato sauce.

Fumble   *Feed the star naked at home, diaper and bib only.*

Feeding your star as she wears just a diaper will save tons of laundry detergent and stain remover. Most guys never use stain remover. Once you have a kid, stain remover is as necessary as a helmet on the football field. Save time and just wash all of your laundry in it. Your star will cover her clothes in a variety of stains. Oh, your clothes will also get covered in food and spit-up.

Quick cleanups on the go are a necessary part of fatherdom; keep a tube of wet wipes in the car. They may be meant for butts, but they are great for cleaning other areas too. A little elbow grease and your star will be as good as new. The head coach probably won't approve, but if the cat is away. . . . Think of cleaning like this as an audible. Audibles are any quick method of doing a baby task that the head coach would never approve of. On-the-field decisions must be made fast.

Audibles *are any quick method of doing a baby task or a choice you have to make quickly without input from the head coach.*

SHOWERS AFTER THE GAME

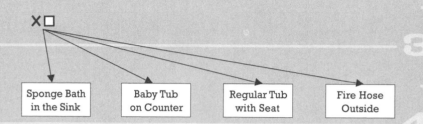

×□

| Sponge Bath in the Sink | Baby Tub on Counter | Regular Tub with Seat | Fire Hose Outside |

EXTRA POINTS

The first baby baths are sponge baths.

A baby tub can be converted to a safety seat in the big tub.

Baths aren't needed every day until they start self feeding.

Volunteer to do the dishes, if you have a dishwasher.

Prepare to be "Caddyshacked" in the bath tub.

At home, feed the baby with her wearing only a diaper.

INJURY TIMEOUTS AND
11. THE TEAM BUS

Baby safety is the number one concern for most QB dads as their little stars get mobile. The head coach will probably leave this task up to you, but she will give you lots of advice. Babyproofing is important, and it is generally going to be your role. Did I mention that the head coach will give you lots of advice? Although you probably won't be the primary healer, we will also discuss sickness and baby health in this chapter.

ATHLETIC TAPE

Before we discuss babyproofing, let me extol the virtues of athletic tape. You know the white tape they use on ankles, fingers, and so on? A few rolls around the house are a must for the QB dad. This stuff is great. Of course, you can also use duct tape for many of the same jobs, but athletic tape comes off skin easier, and white just looks better.

Athletic tape is perfect for saving a diaper once that tab tears off. Those tabs will come off if you pull very hard, and there is no sense in wasting a fresh diaper. If you use cloth diapers, you don't need pins; use tape instead. Also, the tape is perfect for creating your own diaper if you run out of disposables. Two dish towels and tape and you have an instant diaper.

Fixing toys and making socks stay up are a few other great uses. I even heard a story about repairing a gingerbread house with tape and applying frosting right over the tape. And you might need to tape an ankle or two before the kid grows up. Keep a roll at the house and in the diaper bag.

Fumble *Athletic tape has thousands of uses for your little star. You might even want to tape an ankle to help her crawl.*

Of course, in order to use the tape you will have to learn "the tear." The tear is a skill that takes practice. Practice perfecting the art when no one is looking. Fingernails help but are not required. You want to be ready with a perfect tear when called upon. And you don't want to be seen using scissors. Safety scissors to remove tape is okay, but you need to be able to tear it off the roll. Once it folds over and touches itself, give up and get a new piece.

BABYPROOFING THE STADIUM

Babyproofing a house can be simple or complicated. If the head coach reads all of the baby books out there, good luck. They will warn you of every possible scenario. And they will tell you to buy something to make that area safe. Safety is important and agree with the head coach on her wants.

Since your star doesn't become mobile for about six months, this is a job that can be procrastinated. So you have some time to decide what you need to babyproof and how much is needed. My nieces were practically raised in a construction zone and they are great, healthy kids. Our parents probably didn't do much beyond plastic plugs for the outlets and we turned out okay.

Gates

Gates are one item that needs to be agreed upon. We used gates to cordon off some free-to-crawl zones, but we had several friends who did not. Their babies appear to be healthy and normal past year one. Using gates may also depend upon the layout of the house and how often you want to chase the little one down as she bootlegs out of the room.

 A **bootleg** *is the baby crawling out of eyesight.*

Gates come in two varieties: pressure fit and hardware mounted. Pressure fits are easier to use and portable. Hardware-mounted gates have hinges and latches that mount to the wall; they are safer and sturdier. The one area that gates are required for is the top of a staircase, and these need to be hardware mounted for safety. Doors are the best form of baby gate possible. Close doors to the basement, if you have one. Also close doors to bathrooms.

Outlets, Cords, and Kitchen Drawers

Dangling cords are a baby danger. Tuck them behind furniture or roll them up and place out of reach. This includes miniblind cords. Use the plastic outlet plugs for all electrical outlets in baby-safe areas. These plugs can be simple plastic push-in types or complex two-handed types.

Touchdown

The most dangerous area in most houses is under the sink. Move all the chemicals to higher ground.

The kitchen is a major danger area, and you need to be particularly careful here. Cabinet locks need to be installed on all of the lower cabinets. Cabinet locks can be magnetic or manually operated. Move the cleaning supplies to a spot out of the baby's reach. Above the fridge and in the laundry room are options. The most dangerous things in your house are usually under the sink in bright, colorful bottles. They also make locks for the fridge, stove, toilet, and windows.

Playroom

My advice is to create a 100 percent safe zone in at least one room. The television room is a great room to completely babyproof. You want one room in which your star is free to roam and you are free to not worry. Of course, you need to be in the room and alert, but continual eye contact might not be needed. Move all pictures, books, and trophies well out of reach. Be sure the TV cannot be pulled down. Cover the corners of any hard furniture with padding. Place gates at all of the sidelines and put plugs in all of the outlets.

Some level of babyproofing is needed in all rooms where the baby is going to crawl. Get down at baby level and crawl around the room. Make sure you do this at a time the head coach will see you. You are going to look silly, but you will earn major points in the daddy game. Do not let your friends see you unless they are dads also.

HEALTH AND SICKNESS

Baby health will most likely be the head coach's domain, but be prepared to help out. A sick baby is not a pleasant sight, and the sooner she is better, the sooner life can get back to normal.

Fevers are one of the greatest concerns for babies. If the fever elevates above 100.4 degrees, it is probably time to call the experts. Babies don't regulate temperature as easily as we do, and fevers can be dangerous.

Simple colds are a regular visitor to most new babies. You will be amazed at the amount of snot that can come from the tiniest nose in the house. Keep wiping. There are baby medicines out there, but read the directions very carefully. Ask your pediatrician for recommendations. Buy these meds ahead of time; trips to the store at 3 AM are not fun.

Touchdown

Buy the common baby medications ahead of time to avoid middle-of-the-night trips. Only give them to your child after the pediatrician says it's safe to do so.

Colic is a common baby illness that bothers up to a fourth of all babies. Colic is a little-understood disease, even by the experts. Colic will produce three- to four-hour crying fits, where your baby will be inconsolable. The baby will look like she is in pain because she is. Experts seem to think it has to do with the digestive system, but that is all they agree on. Immature digestive system and reflux are the two most common causes blamed. It usually starts at around six weeks and lasts for up to two months. It is usually more upsetting to the parents than the child, since it will result in extended crying bouts for your little star. These bouts usually start in the late afternoon. Your star will still eat and be happy most of the time, but she will cry for hours. Trust me; it will go away. Keep your doctor aware of this and ask him for advice.

Most insurance companies will pay for well-child visits every three months in the first year. It is important to have an expert look over your little star. Try to attend these if possible. Major daddy points are earned by being present. Use this opportunity to ask the doctor any questions you have.

At these visits, they will measure height, weight, and head circumference. The doc will then show you a graph showing how your kid stacks up on all of these measurements. What percentile your child is in will only be an issue if she is at the extremes. The doc will also strip the kid naked and examine all of her body parts. The doctor will ask a few questions and answer yours before he leaves. After he leaves, the evil wicked nurse will deliver any needed shots. Your star could grow to love the doctor but may hate the nurse. You can give children's pain reliever to your star before you go to take the edge off of the vaccine shots. Keep your star up to date on vaccines. Getting the star a flu shot every year might also be a good idea. The head coach may make all of the health decisions for your little star. Make sure you are aware of what is happening and don't be afraid to ask questions. Taking an active role in the health concerns of your baby is of vital importance.

THE TEAM BUS

Jumping into the car for a quick trip to the store gets more involved when your little star is added to the mix. Driving around with your first-round draft pick will take a vehicle larger than your BMW Z3. Safety and a well-stocked car are the keys to short drives with your baby.

Car seat, a stocked diaper bag, and emergency supplies in the car are necessary. All football teams carry spare gear for game emergencies, so should a good QB dad.

Car Seats

Safety is the number one concern anytime you load the little one into the car. A new car seat is a must. Don't buy a used car seat. It may have been in an accident and be weakened. It is not worth the gamble. A hand-me-down seat from a relative could probably be trusted if you trust the relative (and they bought it new).

For the star's first car seat I suggest one of the traveling systems with an integrated carrier. These carriers just snap into the base and away you go. You may want to buy an extra base if both of you will be transporting your star. Short drives won't be this easy again until your star is in a booster seat.

Make sure the car seat has been inspected by a trained expert. Also make sure that you hear and feel it latch into place every time. The straps should be in the correct place and the middle slide should be up over her chest. Never take a chance and carry her without doing all of the straps.

 *A **short drive** is any QB dad car trip that doesn't involve an overnight stay.*

This first seat is rear facing and should be used until your little star reaches twenty pounds and is at least 12 months old. You probably want a mirror installed on the rear seat that will allow you eye contact with the little one. The mirror is bright, colorful, and good entertainment. These are available at all baby stores. You are advised to stay away from toys that hook to the carrier arm.

Touchdown

 Always use a rear-facing car seat until the first Super Bowl and the little star has reached twenty pounds.

After your little star outgrows the carrier, you move up to the next size car seat. These can face front and rear and are usually used when your star weighs between twenty and forty pounds. All new car seats come with several latches. Always latch every one and slide the front snap up high on her chest. Two are in the fold of the seat and the third is behind the seat. The car seat has three latches that connect to all of these hooks. There are metal U-shaped pieces that are integral to your car's own seat. Pull the straps to tighten them. The car seat should not move more than one inch. All seats can also be secured using a shoulder seat belt. *Read the instructions* carefully for installation. Ask your pediatrician for any advice on best types if the head coach doesn't make the decision for you.

They also make convertible seats that will eventually become a booster seat. I'm not sure if they are worth it. By the time the kid reaches forty pounds, the car seat will have had six gallons of milk and three gallons of juice spilled on it. Might be time for a new smell in the car at this time.

Stocking the Car

A diaper bag is a must when you go on a short drive. If the head coach is with you, the diaper bag will never be forgotten. But when you are alone, you will forget it sometimes. Guys just don't have that built-in baby-care gene that the head coach has. For this reason, stash an extra diaper, wet wipes, and a few towels somewhere in the car. A small cylindrical container of wet wipes will be more valuable than you realize. They will allow you to clean up spills and wipe your own hands.

A Larger Bus?

The car will probably grow as your family grows. You might be able to get by with one family car and a sports car. But all transporting would have to be done in the big one. Having two baby-ready cars is helpful in today's rush-around world. If one parent stays at home, you could even get by on one car to save dough. You might as well sell your two-seat sports car. You can always buy another sports car when you go through a midlife crisis, unless you are David Letterman and your midlife crisis is having a kid.

Touchdown

Find out all the local laws on transporting kids before she goes on her first scoring drive.

Short trips around town are easy with almost any sedan, but minivans are nicer for long trips. Minivans get a bad rap in my opinion. They are large and well equipped for convenience. Vans are also nice when the team grows in size. Vans also are convenient when you buy the jumbo boxes of diapers and the gross of batteries you need every Christmas from now on.

Regardless of what car you drive, find out all the local laws on transporting kids. The laws vary from state to state. There are a few guidelines that are always wise.

CAR SAFETY TIPS

1 If possible, place the baby seat in the center of the rear seat. This will allow the baby to be more protected in the event of a fender bender. With many cars, the middle of the back seat is not an option.

2 Kids should be rear facing for the first twelve months and until they reach 20 pounds. This is the safest position for them. The mirror will help you keep an eye on them. And secure all the latches. *Never* let them ride on your lap. Even just across a parking lot is not worth a chance.

INJURY TIMEOUTS

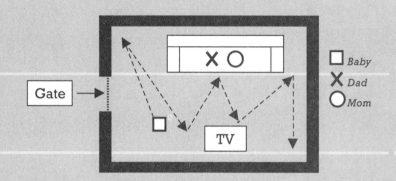

□ Baby
✕ Dad
○ Mom

Gate →

EXTRA POINTS

Babyproofing is important and it is usually the QB dad's job.

Use gates to cordon off some free-to-crawl zones.

The kitchen is a major danger area.

Create a 100 percent safe zone in at least one room.

Crawl around the room and make sure the head coach sees you.

Buy athletic tape for the 1,001 emergencies that will arise.

Go to all well-child visits, if possible.

Take an active, supporting role when the little one is sick.

3 For the future, keep them in the back seat until they are a teenager. This is the law in some states anyway, but it just makes sense. Airbags and seat belts are designed for adults. They can actually be dangerous to a little one. Once they are almost teens, they still may opt for the back seat. That way they can avoid talking to dad.

Safety is the number one concern every time you jump into the car with your little star. Remember to stock your car with an extra diaper and a container of wet wipes. Common sense will go a long way toward making every short drive a scoring short drive.

12. WAYS TO CALM YOUR STAR

Learning how to soothe your number one draft pick is a skill that all QB dads must learn. Music, motion, and various other techniques help make this possible. Besides, once your star finally goes to sleep, you can grab some shuteye yourself.

Rocking, moving, burping (the kid, not you), and even running the vacuum cleaner (which provides a soothing noise, similar to what a kid experiences *in utero*) can all help quiet a fussy child. Skin-to-skin contact is also a great way to get your star to settle down. Take your shirt off as you calm the baby; it worked wonders for me. However, the trick you'll most often use after ruling out the usual suspects (seeing if your kid is tired, wet, or hungry) is music. They say music soothes the savage beast, and at 3 AM your little star may seem pretty savage.

Touchdown

The only way a baby has to communicate with you is to cry.

Babies cry. It's just a fact. They are not crying to make you mad. They cry because they're hungry, wet, bored, and lonely. They may even cry because you have a bad singing voice.

Actually, they don't have a reference for bad singing yet. You will sound like an angel to them. Your college roommates probably know your singing sucks. But your voice will be the sweetest thing your star has ever heard, and it may be several years before she realizes how bad your singing really is.

SING YOUR STAR TO SLEEP

You need to find one song or lullaby to use from day one. Most dads find a song that will comfort and console the little one. Even if you try different songs, it is nice to have an old standby. It's kind of like the Rolling Stones singing "Satisfaction" in concert; it's an old standard that always keeps the audience happy. Your child will eventually associate that song with you and that will comfort her.

Touchdown

You will need at least one song that is a guaranteed hit.

I personally sang the Irish lullaby "Too-ra-loo-ra-loo-ral" to my daughter from day one. Well at least I sang the chorus from this song (that's all I knew). This came from my English grandfather, and it was nice to pass it down in the family. With the Internet, I could actually look up all the lyrics, but I still only sang the chorus. Trust me; it is hard to concentrate at 3 AM. The chorus would almost always calm her as I delivered her to the head coach. Breast-feeding babies are consoled by the head coach much easier; she is better equipped for babies than you.

When kids wake up, they usually want to eat. Patience is a foreign concept to a baby. They want food and they want it five minutes ago. Don't freak out. Just use your standby song to comfort her and get her to the food supply as quickly as possible. The baby will eventually learn to trust that you will make it better. It takes time (a good portion of the first year), but eventually they won't cry for food the moment they wake up.

 Fumble *For breast-feeding babies, boobies will have a more calming effect than your singing.*

As my little star got older, I became more adept at reading her different cries. Babies have a boredom cry, a hunger cry, and a "pick me up, you idiot" cry among others. Other books say babies have a wetness cry, but with today's diapers they don't get wet. They would have to pee about half a gallon to feel any wetness. Better living thorough chemistry.

After about six months I switched to "B-I-N-G-O," mostly just for something different for me, but it worked like a charm. She would instantly quiet down. At about one year, I actually switched to the "A-B-C" song and it also worked like magic. The added benefit was at about seventeen months she could sing the ABCs with people and she looked incredibly smart. The lesson here is that almost any song works. I do feel the comfort of a familiar song works better than continuously changing tunes. Even at two years of age, my daughter still settles down to the Irish lullaby.

Try college fight songs, frat songs, traditional lullabies, and popular music hits. Stay away from Parental Advisory lyrics.

You don't want your star embarrassing you at the age of two. Feel free to experiment to find the perfect baby-soothing melody.

Sing softly in her ear even when she is crying. She will hear enough and the crying will eventually subside, hopefully. Walking while you are singing adds an extra amount of comfort and a change of scenery. Scientists now know that babies are much more aware of their surroundings than was once thought. New things to look at may help her forget why she is crying.

White Noise

It also helps to find a room with a ceiling fan or another source of white noise. Babies are amazed by the gentle spin of a ceiling fan. White noise of almost any type will also soothe and quiet them. Experts say this is a result of being comforted while they were in the womb. The womb is an incredibly noisy place. They heard all the body sounds of the head coach as well as many outside sounds. Blood pumping, stomach rumblings, and gas passing were music to a baby's ears in the womb. Try to imagine how noisy gas must be when you are napping on the intestines. Also, think back to all those times you talked directly to your star through your head coach's stomach. Your star will know your voice before she ever leaves the womb.

Touchdown

White noise generators are great tools for soothing a little one.

One friend of mine actually ran the vacuum to soothe her baby. Two birds with one stone—a cleaner house and happier baby. I have also heard that babies love reggae music. The beat is usually about sixty beats per minute, similar to a heartbeat, so it comforts them.

 Fumble *Tell the head coach that* **SportsCenter** *(or the NFL Channel) makes great background noise.*

You can also buy white noise generators at those fancy stores with the massaging chairs at the mall or online. These will play many different sounds like rain, a babbling brook, and even a heartbeat. My daughter used one to nap to and it usually worked well. It will also cover up the noise coming from your favorite game. Early on, your star will nap through anything. However, as your baby gets older, you may find she wakes up more easily. As my daughter approached one year, she would be startled awake by any sudden, loud noise. The background noise helped. I have a friend who created white noise by leaving the television on all the time. He would ignore the television set until he heard keywords like football, bank robbery, and swimsuit model. Let's face it; the constant drivel of most television stations is white noise to you and me.

BABY GAS

Gas in the baby will also cause your star to be fussy. Sometimes all it takes is a good burp to quiet your star. That is something that all QB dads can relate to. Think about how good a healthy burp makes you feel after a big meal. Your kid may just be a chip off the old block.

As all guys know, there are two ways to get gas out of your body, and the same goes for a baby. Butt gas from a baby makes everybody laugh, except when it's hurting the baby. During these times, you can use the gas pump method. Lay your star on his back and push his knees up toward his chest. Two or three pumps and the gas will usually come out. They also make gas drops, but that is not as much fun as the gas pump.

MOTION

Motion is another method you can try to calm down your star. Pacing and using a rocking chair are two methods that will usually have success. Gliders have the added benefit of not smashing little fingers as they get mobile. Most people I know either swear by the glider and use it often or use it as a storage device for clothes.

Most QB dads will pace over five hundred miles in the first year. A nice leisurely walk will calm many babies. You might have to replace the carpet in your hallway someday, but that is a cheap price to pay for getting your star to sleep. Pacing while singing works great. Some QB dads learn how to be a triple threat: They can pace, sing, and burp their star at the same time.

Sometimes a car ride is the only way to soothe your star. Car rides put most kids to sleep. A car ride provides motion

MUSIC IN THE STADIUM

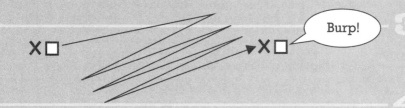

Rocking, walking, burping, and a vacuum cleaner can calm a newborn.

Babies do not cry to make you mad.

Find a single song that will comfort and console the little one.

Switch songs occasionally, but the baby will have a favorite.

Boobies may have a more calming effect than your singing.

Patience is a foreign concept to a baby.

The womb is an incredibly noisy place, so use noise to calm your star.

and white noise at the same time. With the price of gas so high, this should only be a last-ditch effort. I had a friend who took his daughter to see the "flying fish" at a local lake every night for a three-month period. The fish jumped during the day and his daughter loved watching them. I don't think they jumped at night, but she was asleep by the time he reached the lake. Once around the lake, then he would return to the house and carry her in to her crib.

 Motion *can be sending a WR across the formation or pacing the house with your little star.*

Experiment to find what it takes for your superstar; you will find some combination that works for a period of time. Your star will realize that you are going to fix whatever is wrong and she will settle down faster. Music, motion, and white noise are all tried and true methods of calming the little one. And never underestimate the power of a good burp.

KEEPING THE HEAD COACH
13. HAPPY

In the daddy game, the importance of a happy head coach can never be underestimated. This chapter contains hints on how to get some me time and make the head coach happy. Keeping her happy helps the entire team function more smoothly. In addition to her happiness, don't neglect the importance of your own happiness.

CREATING A HAPPY TEAM

A happy team contributes to a well-adjusted child. Your star will sense any unease and strife between you and the head coach. Babies are much more aware of what is happening around them than people realize. Keeping the house chaos to a minimum will lessen this strife. This is a difficult task when both of you are sleep deprived.

Touchdown

Studies show that frequent hugging leads to happy, healthier babies.

Don't we all want a sweet, good-natured baby? Creating one is going to be a function of how the both of you deal with being blind-sided. Somewhere between zero and sixty-eight times a day, you are going to do something to annoy the head coach. On the flip side, she will tick you off just as much. Try to remember that you both have the same goal. She doesn't forget something on purpose just to make you mad. You need to be extra flexible with a newborn in the house. Ranting and raving will not accomplish anything. Also, try not to bring your work home with you. Focus on your family when you are home.

Head Coach Types

You both need some me time. Encourage her to get it first. Remember, she just pushed a football through her birth canal. She may need to be pried away from your first-round draft pick, but it will be great for her. Moms appear to fall into two different types. The two types are the man-to-man cornerback mom and free safety mom.

 *The **man-to-man cornerback** moms will never let the baby out of their sight. They will refuse all offers of baby-sitting.*

The man-to-man cornerback mom never wants to let the baby out of her sight. These moms really don't want me time and might be offended at the suggestion. You need to suggest that she go out anyway. She needs to interact with other adults and maybe other moms. A play group may be a good compromise. She will have a chance to keep an eye on the star and get hints from other moms while spending time out of the house with other adults.

Be aware that you will be compared to other dads. If you are helpful and supportive in baby things, this will be good. She will appreciate all of your talents and hard work. You can increase the chance of being looked at favorably by using good clock management. This involves being extra helpful for the few days leading up to a play group or any other outing. Of course, you should always try to be helpful. But just like in football, timing is crucial. A slip up before play group will result in a larger penalty.

N F L *You can increase the chance of being looked at favorably by using **good clock management**. Choose when to be extra helpful to maximize the benefits.*

The free safety mom will gladly take up any offer of babysitting. Like a free safety, she will allow others to watch over your star and will be there if needed. She may even demand some me time first. This does not make her any less of a mom. All moms have their own level of comfort with someone else watching their child. She may want (and need) a mom's night out without the star. The head coach will arrive home happy and refreshed. This leads to a smoother household. By the way, you will still be compared to other dads. I think all head coaches compare quarterbacks when they are together.

ONE-ON-ONE TIME WITH YOUR STAR

Take on the sole responsibility of watching the star while the head coach takes time to do a hobby, has dinner with adult friends, and so on. Man-on-man defense is actually empowering for you and great for the kid. As a QB dad, you will fall into ease with your star and alone time will become painless. You don't do things the same way as the head coach, but that is okay. The earlier you keep the baby by yourself, the better. Remember, for the first six months your baby is immobile and only eats, sleeps, and fills diapers. Use this time to get used to being alone with the little one. Your dad may have never watched you on his own, but wouldn't you like to be better than him? It also helps to have the head coach bragging about you to her friends.

Solo Missions with the Baby

Taking the baby out is a great way to amuse both of you. Baby trips for the first year will vary by age. Make sure all of the places you visit are smoke free and relatively quiet. Everybody thinks of zoos, parks, museums, and malls, but there are plenty of other options. Great trips for the zero to six-month-old crowd are supermarkets, pet stores, and big box superstores. Volunteering to go to the supermarket will qualify you for the QB dad Hall of Fame. Supermarkets are full of bright colors and people to amuse your star. Pet stores are cheap places to go, if you can resist buying an animal. Big box superstores are great and you might get some stuff you need. My star loves the home improvement store, and the electronic superstore contains movies, video games, and music to amaze her. Never take a trip to the department store without a trip to the aquarium. The tanks of fish stuffed back in the corner of the store will keep her amused for up to an hour.

During the second half of her first year you can add some new destinations. Dog parks, construction sites, lakes, casinos, and football practices all work once your star gets mobile. Many towns have dog parks, but use care with strange dogs. Parking the stroller outside the fence and carrying the baby in your arms is a good, safer alternative. Large construction sites will usually have big machinery, and you can stay in the car for a nice view. Lakes, oceans, and ponds will allow you to feed the fish and/or ducks. Ducks love day-old bread. If you go in the nonsmoking side of a casino, it will actually be a baby heaven. But be aware that your star may start betting her lunch money when she starts school.

Touchdown

 Taking the baby out (without the head coach) is great for you and the baby.

Football practices are the perfect place to bond with your star. Most pro and college teams have open practices early in the season that will probably be closed later. You can almost always go see a high-school team practice in the afternoon or youth league at night. The movement, whistles, and bright colors will bring a smile to your first-round draft pick. You will be told that you can't use a video camera during team periods, but everything else will be fine. Many players will smile and wave at your first-round draft pick. Taking your baby on a mini road trip is a great way to entertain both of you.

Once you have mastered taking care of the baby by yourself, it is okay to take the baby over to mom's or the in-law's house. Make sure that you have done it a few times solo before using the assistant coaches. If you run over to their houses each time you are alone with the star, you won't get any credit for being helpful. The head coach will assume that mom is doing all the work.

ME TIME

Your head coach will return the favor and let you get out for a poker night, football game, golf game, or to do whatever your hobby is. It is healthy for you to still have guy friends. Just make sure that going out with the guys is limited in both length and frequency. You want a healthy relationship with the head coach, so be considerate. Being friends with other new dads may help, as they understand the importance of being a good QB dad. Don't abuse me time. Find a comfort level with the head coach.

Always overestimate your return time. When you take off to watch the big game with the guys, tell her you will be home at 1 AM, and then when you show up at the house at midnight she is happy. She doesn't have to know all the other dads had to be home at midnight also. Underestimating your return time will cause problems for your team. You can reset all the clocks in the house, but that didn't work in high school and won't work now. If you have a few brews, designate a backup quarterback to get you home safely.

Touchdown

Always overestimate your return time by one to two hours.

With team finances being important, be frugal with your nights out. A nickel ante poker game is just as much fun as a higher stakes game. When it comes to games, for cheap tickets head for the end zone. The best season tickets that I ever had were in the end zone. The end zone fans are fun; they boo and cheer with passion. And cheap tickets allow more money for hot dogs, beer, and whatever else you want at the game. Of course, you need to take the star to a few games, but no beer if the star is with you. Maybe you can indulge in one, so the kid can learn about moderation, but *never* drink and drive.

SCORING MAJOR DADDY POINTS

Being thoughtful around the house is another way to keep your team running smoothly. Try to do small chores without being asked. Taking down the trash before it overflows is guaranteed to score points in the daddy game. Whisk the little one off for a bath when the head coach has had a hard day. On a really bad head coach day, fire up the grill and cook dinner. Even guys that can't cook can grill. There is just something about cooking over open flame that brings out the best in dads.

Small gifts can earn more points than expensive jewelry, unless you give them on a holiday. A small gift on Valentine's Day or a birthday will result in a trip to the doghouse. The small gifts I am talking about are cards, notes, a candy bar, or a single flower. Give them for no reason. Mail a mushy card to your head coach where she works, even if it is at home. Sneak a Post-it note in her purse with a sweet saying on it. Hide her favorite chocolate somewhere in the house where she will find it. Don't hide chocolate in the diaper pail. She will find it, but she will probably bench you.

Prolonged Mood Swings

On a very serious note, after the baby is born some women will suffer from postpartum depression (PPD). This is a very serious condition and needs to be treated as such. Watch for crying fits, lack of pleasure in favorite activities, sleeping problems, and more. This is not to be confused with the baby blues. The baby blues are common in the first few days after birth and will usually go away in a few days or weeks. But PPD can happen anytime in the first year. PPD will be longer and more involved than a few weeks.

Experts now know that it is legitimate and needs to be treated. Have an open dialogue with the head coach about it. She can't just "snap out of it," and it is no one's fault. Don't blame yourself (or her). PPD is a natural occurrence that may affect up to a fifth of all new moms. Go to all doctor's appointments with her. Take this very seriously. You can help by doing anything that reduces her stress. Taking over a few more feedings, doing additional cooking and cleaning, and providing good family time will all help but may not be enough. She may need professional help. You should call her doctor if you grow concerned. PPD can and should be treated.

Touchdown

Small gifts for no reason score big points in the daddy game.

A sure-fire way to win the daddy game is to buy her a gift on your little star's first birthday. Put a note in it thanking her for being a great mom. You will be the envy of the play group. Call her cell phone and leave a sweet (or racy) message when you know she won't answer it. She'll get it later and smile. A smiling head coach will be more likely to give you some playing time.

Playing Time

While on the subject of playing time, here are a few observations. The head coach may be a mom, but she is still a woman. She wants to be wanted. Treat her like you were still dating. Keep romance alive in your bedroom. Sleep deprivation may lessen the urges, but romance can win some back. Light a few candles before she enters the room. If she just walks over and blows them out, you know where you stand. If she says "that's sweet," she is allowing you to go on offense first. Start with a nice, controlled opening drive. Don't throw deep on the first play. If she grabs you and starts to kiss you, she is on offense. I love defense.

ROAD TRIPS

Long trips will help break up a long home stand. Going away with the baby is like a football team traveling to a bowl game: It takes lots of planning and a semi truck. Since most of us don't own a semi, careful planning is needed.

The head coach will probably act as the equipment manager for your team. She will do this because she doesn't trust you. She knows you will forget something, and she also knows you are comfortable with that. Your stories of weeklong spring break trips with only a single duffle bag are burned into her memory.

 N F L *For long trips, the head coach will serve as the* **equipment manager.**

Most guys pack quick and light. We know that wherever we are going has stores in case we forget anything. We also know that we can borrow anything needed from our friends. Most women don't understand this. The thought of sharing a razor or bathing suit appalls them. Ninety-nine percent of guys never bring extra clothes. We count the days and pack accordingly. A three-day trip means sandals, sneakers, three pairs of socks, three tees, one pair of shorts, one bathing suit, and one pair of jeans. Well, maybe we bring one nice shirt and a toothbrush. Everything else can be borrowed or bought. This is the reason we only need one duffle bag. Guys will also throw a Frisbee, football, and basketball directly into the car.

Packing for the Baby

Traveling with a baby requires the largest suitcase ever made. We have a suitcase that was designed for a month-long vacation. It is the perfect size for one week's worth of one newborn's clothing. The suitcase will have all of these neat little pockets that the equipment manager will love to fill up. I own a Nike hit man duffle bag, but it gets vetoed because it doesn't have all the neat pockets. My advice is to leave the room while she packs for the little one. You can use your old duffle bag for her food, toys, and books, which won't fit in the suitcase.

Logic will make no sense as she packs. She will pack a minimum of three outfits per day. She will also take every pair of shoes that fit, even before your star can walk. She will take every color of baby sock that you own. Even if you are going to South Beach in July, she will still pack a sweater, jacket, and gloves.

Touchdown

For a three-day trip, you will pack every article of clothing that fits your little star.

If you have a daughter with hair, every color of headband and hair clip must also leave the house. Bald daughters are easier to pack for; you only need three elastic headbands. These are required to keep people from guessing the gender of your star. Let's face it; for the first year color-coded clothes and headbands are the only way to tell the sex of a newborn.

You have changed her diaper; other people haven't. Of course, screwing with people by dressing your daughter in blue is fun. I always approach strange babies with "What a beautiful baby" unless they have given an obvious clue.

You will probably be put in charge of toys; the head coach won't trust you with clothes or food. She knows you are a guy, so she may trust you with toys. Grab a few age-appropriate toys and take some books. Leave a few toys in the car to entertain your star during the drive.

The portable crib will be a big help once you reach your destination, or you can let the little one sleep with you. Another nice travel help is a portable high chair/booster seat. These will turn any chair into a high chair. We leave one in the car when visiting friends and relatives.

Loading the Team Bus

Here is where a minivan helps. You will probably have all of the following to load: portable crib, travel system stroller, one gigantic suitcase for the baby's clothes, one large suitcase for the head coach's clothes, one large duffle of toys, one large duffle of baby food, a cooler, and your tiny duffle bag. It will take an engineering degree to fit this into a smaller vehicle. And pray that the head coach doesn't scrapbook, knit, or have any other space-consuming hobby to travel with.

There are a few ways to accomplish the mission if you own a car smaller than a semi. One, rent a semi, or at least a bigger vehicle. This may be expensive, but it makes packing easier. Two, buy a rooftop car carrier. These are not only attractive but also useful. If you are going to take a lot of trips, buying one is the way to go. They come both hard and soft sided. The soft-sided carriers are cheaper and good ones are waterproof. We own a heavyweight vinyl carrier that withstood the rain from a hurricane. You can also borrow a carrier from friends; check with a friend that skis or snowboards.

After three or so trips you will be looking for a larger car. We bought a minivan at my urging. I was tired of trying to put ten pounds of stuff in a five-pound bag. I am selling my rooftop carrier if anyone is interested. The minivan is nice, but if we have a second kid I will need to go larger. Maybe I can buy a surplus military truck.

Baby Distractions

Pack the front seats of the car with all manner of baby distraction tools, animal puppets, big colorful picture books, and all types of music. Mother Goose, lullaby, Sesame Street, and early Beatles CDs all are helpful. Turn off her music as soon as your star is asleep. Trust me, you will hear them enough when she is awake.

Touchdown

Pack the front of the car with lots of distractions for the baby. Keep baby snacks that can be eaten in the car close at hand.

We own a Winnie the Pooh ABC CD that I heard 1,657,812 times by the time my daughter turned one. A mix CD containing all-time great sing-along songs is also a hit. "Friends in Low Places," "Respect," "Come on Eileen," "Shake Your

Booty," "My Girl," and all the other songs we know by heart are all great choices. Tailor the list to your taste, but give the little one a variety.

Plugging in a video when traveling in the car can be an easy way to calm your star, but I think this is cheating. Your star needs to learn patience, and long, boring car trips are the best place to teach them. Think back to all of the boring trips with your parents; they helped prepare you for staff training meetings at work. We bought a minivan without a DVD player, but those are getting harder to find. A friend of mine has a three-hour rule. He allows the kids to watch a video after they have been in the car for, you guessed it, three hours. That seems like a fair compromise to me, but we still don't own a video player for the car. On the interstate, I admit that I drive next to cars playing movies to give my daughter a peek and then I add the dialogue.

Driving at Night

The baby will sleep more than normal when you are traveling during the day. So if you travel during the day, this could mean a restless night once you reach your destination. Driving at night is an option that has been used by many of my friends. Even with Mountain Dew, caffeine pills, and chocolate, I can't do it. But many people can, and with young kids it can be beneficial. You won't screw up their sleep patterns, but it might take you a couple of days to recuperate. It also gives you more time to spend on vacation if you are driving. You don't lose valuable play days, which is especially important if your schedule is tight. For the safety of the entire team, exercise extreme caution if you do this. A compromise is to drive until midnight and then get a hotel room. It costs a few dollars but gives you more fun time.

Touchdown

If driving, take frequent breaks so the little one gets a chance to move around.

Traveling by car with a little one is a daunting task. But newborns are easier to travel with than tweens. By the time we reach that point, we will probably have a video player and all the kids will have headphones, iPods, and portable game systems. Not every QB dad needs to hear "Are we there yet?" several hundred times in his lifetime. You can survive a car trip with your star.

The Team Charter

Plane trips are faster, but they bring their own problems. Up to a certain age the baby can usually fly for free on most carriers, but she will have to sit in your lap. The safest route is to buy a ticket and use a car seat. Some airlines may let you use a car seat in an empty seat if there are any. Check with the airline first for its policies and rules.

If she flies with you, the entire plane is part of the entertainment for the baby. Encourage people to smile, wave, and play peekaboo with your star. If she is happy, everybody's flight will be better.

Babies are more susceptible to air pressure differences, so a bottle or a pacifier is recommended when taking off and landing. Small snack foods may also work for older babies. You probably know how to make your eardrums pop, but your star doesn't. Nursing on airplanes is a hot debate, and some airlines have even kicked mothers off of flights for nursing. Call and ask the airline you are traveling on to find out its policy regarding breast-feeding while on one of its planes.

Get on the plane last, if possible. The little one will have to spend the flight in a confined area, so give him the shortest time possible. If you have a lot of carryon stuff, you might want to board earlier or have the head coach board earlier while you wait outside.

Once you reach your destination, you will need to babyproof the room. Most hotel rooms are indestructible, but get on your hands and knees and check it out. Put suitcases in front of any potential hazards. Once your little one gets older, disconnect the phone as soon as you get in the room.

 Fumble *Even on vacation, the QB dad is still in charge of babyproofing.*

Taking trips is fun and a great way to see the world. Vacations become different once you have kids. You see things in a whole new way. Enjoy and travel safely.

TOUCHDOWNS AND FIELD GOALS

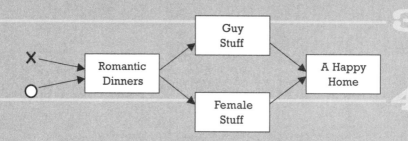

Keep the head coach happy; the entire team runs better.

You both need some alone time for a healthy relationship.

Baby-sit to earn points and bond with your star.

Always overestimate your return time when you go on an outing.

Be thoughtful around the house.

Small gifts for no reason score big points in the daddy game.

Good teamwork will help the entire team function.

PLAYING DEFENSE DURING THE
14. HOLIDAYS

Holidays with a baby bring many new joys and maybe a few unexpected terrors into your life. Parties are still fun, you just need a different game plan than in the old days. You will probably start decorating more for the holidays than before. Assembling toys may bring a newfound respect for your parents.

Keeping up with the baby at holidays and Super Bowl parties is a skill all QB dads must learn. Many people absolutely love babies, so this might be easier than you think. Holidays with a little one will bring many smiles and allow you to share the joy, but they also bring a little terror to the QB dad as well. You will probably gain a newfound respect for your own QB dad after your first major fall holiday.

Babies cause most people to smile. And getting other people to smile can be your way of improving the world. Of course, there are a few baby scrooges. Baby scrooges are put off and offended by little ones. My best advice is to avoid these people. Since baby scrooges are a very small percentage of all people, they are easy to avoid.

HOLIDAY PARTIES

During the holiday season you will be invited to many parties. Go, enjoy, and take the baby to share the wealth of smiles she will bring. Baby scrooges will have parties; get a baby sitter for those parties where children aren't allowed. Most parties will welcome the kids, and little ones are encouraged to come. You might want to leave them home at five or six years of age, but babies are great party fun. At parties, my favorite game to play is Pass the Baby, but be aware she will be passed back when she stinks.

Before you get to a party, decide with the head coach whether you are going man-to-man or zone defense. In a man-to-man defense, one of you will be responsible for the kid at a time. This duty can rotate as the evening progresses, but one of you will stay near the baby at all times. Agree on a set rotation schedule ahead of time. While you have baby duty, you are responsible for taking care of baby needs, like food and Mr. Stinky. Remember, it is illegal procedure to hand back a stinky child to your head coach. A man-to-man defense will allow one of you to mingle freely and get into deeper conversations.

When you get relieved from baby duty, it will be your chance to watch the game or argue about which team is better. Many head coaches won't allow the baby out of their sight anyway. These are the man-to-man cornerback moms we discussed earlier. If your head coach is one of these, man-to-man is your only choice at parties. Or should I say woman-to-baby defense? The benefit of this type of head coach is that she doesn't trust you, so you get to spend the entire evening watching the game and arguing about which team is better. The baby will never be more than six feet away from the head coach with this type of mom.

Touchdown

Choose a man-to-man or zone defense for baby patrol at parties.

You can also use a zone defense at parties. In a zone, you are usually both in the room, but the little one will be passed from guest to guest all over the room. You will be able to see the baby across the room and hear her cries, and if Mr. Stinky pays a visit you can spring into action. Upon arriving, make a quick presnap read of any potential baby hazards. In the zone defense, it is important to strategically locate yourself. You need to be able to cover all of the easy escape routes. You also might need to be able to defend low bookcases that contain breakable objects. Think of yourself as a deep safety in a cover three zone.

For the first six months this is usually minimized because the star will only be handed off between people. As the baby gets mobile, presnap reads must get better and quicker. Your star has already broken every glass item she could reach at your house, but you will be invited to at least one holiday party thrown by a person who is a collector. Good luck! If they collect Hummel figurines, don't go. Replacing what your star breaks will cost you your life savings.

**N
F
L** *Always use a **presnap read** to look for baby dangers in a new stadium.*

One way to avoid baby dangers is to host parties. If your house is built for socializing, this may be the way to go. Having parties at home gives you a home-field advantage. Just make sure that the people you invite are bringing most of the food. You don't need any extra duties with a little one in the house. Home-field advantage also allows you to put the baby to sleep in her own locker room and party longer.

 Staying at home for the holidays gives you **home-field advantage** *because your house is already babyproofed.*

You can always scout the locale of the party by asking friends first. If they have little kids you are probably safe. That is almost like playing a football game on a neutral field; it is not the worst place to play. Going into a hostile stadium takes more effort and planning.

At almost all parties you will find a possession receiver (PR) for your baby. This person absolutely loves babies. The PR will hold, hug, and feed the baby and may even want to change a diaper. These are usually women but don't have to be. They are generally people who have never had a baby around or people whose kids are older and long for the smell of baby powder. The PR will be stingy with the baby and not want to share the baby. This person can make your party easier for you.

In your circle of friends, you will quickly find out who the scrooges and the PRs are. Treat the PRs like gold. You are doing them a favor by loaning them a baby, and they are usually trustworthy. Watch them the first few times from a good zone position. Once they have earned the head coach's trust, you can let them go. My head coach and I belong to a monthly supper club. We get together for potluck dinners and conversation. We have already scouted the people at these parties several times. They are trustworthy and we can relax since there are three loving PRs.

People that absolutely love babies are the **possession receivers** *of the football world, sure-handed and trustworthy.*

Understand who the scrooges are and don't judge them harshly. They have either never had kids or let their own head coach do all the work. This doesn't make them bad people. You will even find scrooges who are married to a PR. If they have a baby, the PR probably never let the scrooge near the baby, so babies make them uncomfortable. Scrooges are usually male but don't have to be. If your boss is a scrooge, you may want a baby sitter for the office Christmas party. Many scrooges don't mind kids at all, as long as they are ten feet away at all times.

LIGHTING UP THE NEIGHBORHOOD

Holidays also bring a few new QB dad duties, such as more outside decorations for the house and assembling toys. The head coach may require additional lights, blow-ups, and kids' decorations for the outside of the house. One day will gradually be converted into a decoration day for the outside. Maneuver this day onto a Saturday between the college football regular season and the bowl games. This corresponds to late November or early December, which is perfect for Christmas or Hanukkah decorating.

Fumble *Once you have kids, the outside of your house will turn into a halftime show complete with tons of lights and decorations.*

By the time your star enters school, your house may be a power drain on the neighborhood. At the rate we are gaining lights and decorations, our house will be visible from the space station within three years. The neighbors don't seem to mind, as long as the lights are turned off at 10 PM so they can finally go to sleep. Older neighbors will actually think it is cute. But, most importantly, your little star will love it. All of the lights give you the added bonus of making your house easier to find for the pizza guy. "Just drive toward the glow on the horizon." It will be lit up like a high-school stadium on Friday night during football season.

SOME ASSEMBLY REQUIRED

When it comes to holidays, the words "Some assembly required" scare the hell out of me. Most boxes list the tools needed on the outside. If it needs more than two tools to assemble, steer the head coach to another toy. You will probably be assembling these toys at midnight, so they need to be easy to put together. To be on the safe side, buy a gross of AAA, AA, C, and D batteries before you start assembling. At 1 AM on holiday eves, only overpriced inconvenience stores will be open. We tried to avoid many electronic toys, but today it is hard. People are going to give you electronic toys anyway, so you will need batteries after opening presents. Only veteran parents will include the needed batteries. If you don't have batteries for a toy, make sure it is opened in the middle of all of the chaos. It can be pushed to the side and replaced with another more dazzling toy.

Touchdown

You might want to avoid toys that have the words "Some assembly required" on the box.

I am embarrassed to admit that I now read the directions. It used to be fun to see if you could assemble things by looking at the picture, but at midnight directions are needed. Important advice: Throw out any leftover parts before the head coach sees them. If the head coach sees extra parts, she will insist that you rebuild the toy. Usually there will be extra parts included and you will miss an occasional part. If the toy still functions, no one has to know. I hide all the extra parts in my garage. By the time she is ten, I estimate I will have enough parts to build my own computer.

Fumble *When assembling toys, throw away any extra parts before the head coach sees them.*

After assembling toys when I should be sleeping, I have gained admiration for my dad. Building a swingset under cover of darkness couldn't have been easy. Since my dad is now retired, maybe he can build my daughter her first swing-set. It might be wise to use a helper to assemble toys, especially if your helper enjoys it. You have already earned your way into the new dad fraternity by now anyway; delegating tasks won't cause them to take away your frat pin.

Holidays are a wonderful way to share your little star and grow closer to her. Start a family tradition and buy her one football gift every fall. Enjoy these early holidays; the gifts will be loved and appreciated. When she is thirteen, nothing will be right with any of her gifts. When she reaches this age, buy gifts that you like. At least that will save you a trip to the return counter.

In the first few years you will create many happy memories during the holiday season for your team. Your star will be the hit of most holiday parties and cause many people to smile. The neighbors will also get a laugh out of your house as your decorations grow through the years.

PLAYING DEFENSE

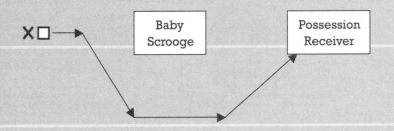

If allowed, take the baby to holiday parties with you.

Most people absolutely love babies.

Try to ignore baby scrooges.

Decide on a man-to-man or zone defense before the party.

You can host parties to gain a home-field advantage.

Look for possession receivers at parties to hold your star.

When you assemble presents, hide leftover parts from the head coach.

You may want to consider reading the assembly directions.

PUTTING THE
BACKFIELD IN MOTION
15. AND CALLING PLAYS

Watching your star grow the first year has been a tremendous joy. The first struggles to open her eyes are a distant memory now. Lying still is also a distant memory. She is moving more and more every day.

TUMMY TIME

Babies need to spend some supervised time on their belly. This will allow her arms to develop the strength needed to push herself up. Since babies now spend most of their early months on their back, babies learn this skill later in life. Put her down on a blanket and watch her strain to lift her head. Keep a close eye on her, and always do this on a firm surface.

Touchdown

Lifting the head is the baby's first step to rolling over.

She will valiantly lift her head to take a look around. The first battle to roll over will be greeted with cheers from her legions of adoring fans. The progression of movement skills is a welcome sight for most QB dads. QB dads long to play catch and wrestle with their own little star. Rolling over is the first step to going out in the yard and tossing the old pigskin.

CRAWLING

Learning to crawl will come during the second half of the first year. Crawling is a skill that happens in stages. It is also a skill that many kids don't master very well. If your baby struggles to crawl, she may walk earlier. Some babies who crawl extremely well see no need to walk. They have managed to get around their world on all fours.

 *The* **four-point stance** *is sometimes the first step to crawling.*

Our star started to get up on all fours at about six months of age, but she never used her knees. She would get into a four-point stance like a defensive lineman on the goal line. Her arms though were not strong enough to lift and move her. She would get up and launch herself forward in a perfect goal-line lunge. The problem was that she invariably landed on her nose. She would struggle back up and do it again. She was determined to get across the room. She sucked at crawling but walked early. Her best friend would scoot across the floor at tailback speed using her own version of crawling. My baby will probably be a 3-4 noseguard plugging up the holes, while her best friend will be a linebacker flying to the tackle.

Don't stress too much about her moving ability in the first year. All kids are different and develop at their own rate. No kid goes to elementary school still crawling. Besides, once they master walking, you will spend several years chasing them.

CRUISING

Walking gets serious when your little one starts using furniture (or the hair on your leg) to pull herself upright. This will lead to a stage called cruising. Cruising is walking with the help of some support. In many houses, a little one will be able to cover large distances based on where the furniture is located. Many kids see no need to venture out without support.

The advantages to a babyproofed room become evident when your little one starts cruising. You can strategically locate furniture to allow him to cruise the entire room in complete safety. Remember that they are going to fall, so make sure all furniture corners are padded. If the room is gated from the rest of the house, you can sit down, rest, and watch your star in action.

Many people swear by the toys that will assist with walking, such as push toys that roll as the baby walks. Make sure that you keep a close eye on her if you use a walking toy, or she will bootleg out of sight. You will be amazed how fast your star can move using a rolling support toy. A large push toy in the middle of the floor will help prepare you for the next few years when your house will become overrun with toys. Never use these toys above the first floor, since a fall down the stairs can cause head injuries.

WALKING

Our star took her first unaided steps the day she turned nine months. I have been chasing her ever since. The old adage of being careful what you wish for is valid. After she starts walking, there will be no more uninterrupted games on television.

Watching her take her first steps will be one of the memorable moments of her first or second year. As with all baby milestones, try to have the video camera there to record the occasion.

What Goes Up Must Come Down

Babies are going to fall approximately a million times in the first year of walking. You might even want to keep count. They will manage to hit every surface in your house that is less than two feet from the floor. Make sure all of these surfaces are safe. Your star will not develop the ability to use her hands to stop falling until well into the second year. That means every time she falls she will be left with a bruise.

My star always managed to hit her forehead. From the age of nine months on she had at least one purple mark on her forehead. It even reached the point where when you said "boo-boo" she would point to her forehead. We have many wonderful baby shots that would never make the cover of *Parents* magazine because of the bruise. In the digital age you can actually learn how to save these pictures and remove the bruise. I really wondered if people (at least the people that never had kids) in the grocery store were going to call Children's Services to report us. Once you have kids, you realize bruises are just a fact of kid life. I know my star is ready for the bruises she will get playing football.

When kids fall they have two advantages that adults don't enjoy: diapers and shortness. Your star will be walking away and all of a sudden take a seat in the middle of a stride. Diapers are a built-in padding to cushion the fall. You can think of diapers as hip pads and a girdle—extra padding for the butt. The other advantage kids have when they fall is their height. They are only going to fall eighteen inches or so. You might get a little bruise from that height but probably not any serious damage. Because of their height, pro football players can do serious damage by falling, but not your little star. A word of caution: Discourage your star from walking on the bed, sofas, and other furniture. You will lose the shortness advantage.

WALKING WITH YOUR STAR

Staying in shape for the baby is of the utmost importance. After all, when she's sixteen you need to be able to intimidate potential boyfriends. Include your star in the activities that you do. Walking is great exercise and a great way to show the little one off. Grab your stroller and away you go. Neighbors will stop you when you are out for a walk with the little one. They may talk to you, but they really just want to see the baby. Blend into the background and let them "goo-goo" away at your little star. This is a great way to bond with the neighbors and maybe scout out some future baby sitters.

If you like maximum mobility, buy a hiking backpack that is designed for kids. They make all kinds of these, but most have a metal frame, a comfy kid seat, and padded straps. Heck, they make them with sunshades, air conditioning, and drink holders. My only advice for using a hiking backpack is wear a hat or else you will be bald before your time as your star will rip every single last hair from your head. These backpacks are really great if you want to go off-road and hit the trails; they can go places strollers can't.

Buy a jogging stroller for an uninterrupted walk. Jogging strollers look like a giant three-wheeled monstrosity. If you like to tinker, you probably could build one out of your old BMX bike and an umbrella stroller. Neighbors won't stop the big-wheeled strollers; they know you mean business. Put an earbud in your ear and pretend you don't hear them if they do try to stop you.

You can also get a frontpack to carry your star in, but good luck. Unless your head coach helps you put it on, you will pull a muscle trying to get into it. The head coach will effortlessly slide it on while you end up in a tangled mess lying on the ground when you try alone. Babybjörn, one of the popular name-brand frontpacks, means "only women can put these on" in Swedish.

Getting more mobile is one of the challenges of the first year. Enjoy watching your little one. By the age of eighteen months, struggling to walk and falling down will be distant memories. Cherish this time, but don't try to rush it. All babies walk once they are able.

BACKFIELD IN MOTION

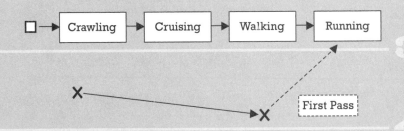

☐ → | Crawling | → | Cruising | → | Walking | → | Running |

X ──────────→ X ⇢ Running

[First Pass]

Crawling is the first step to throwing a football in the yard.

Place the baby on a firm surface to let him lift his head.

If your star struggles to crawl, she might walk earlier.

Push toys and couches are great aids as they learn to walk.

Don't worry too much if they walk late; all babies are different.

Once your star starts walking, you start chasing.

Use a camcorder to record early attempts at walking.

As you approach the end of year one, your little star will begin getting more vocal. She will search for new ways to communicate. Cries will be replaced by sounds, sounds that mean something to her and are supposed to mean something to you.

First Words

Crying was her primary means of communication for at least the first six to nine months. Now she will start repeating words to you. You and the head coach will probably be in a race to get her to say "ma" or "da" first. Good luck.

If you have ever been around other little kids, you probably wondered in amazement how their parents appear to know what they were saying. Now you are beginning to get it. As you spend hours with your star, you realize she says certain words the same. You may not know what she is saying yet, but you will. The baby knows what she is saying. By ten or eleven months, you are the stupid one who can't understand.

 N **F** **L** *If audibles are you making calls at the line of scrimmage,* **inaudibles** *are your star's first attempt at words.*

Babies will repeat what they hear. It took us six months to realize that "daboo, daboo, daboo" was actually "diaper, diaper, diaper." I would repeat it back to her as I headed toward the changing table but was unaware that she was saying it to me.

Baby Talk

Babies will say things in a silly manner. These first attempts at new words will make you laugh. A few will be immortalized as your little star grows up. We all have some words that our parents still laugh at even after we've moved on to three-syllable words. Experts say you should just talk correctly and not repeat mispronounced words. Well, the experts have no sense of humor. The head coach said I was making fun of my star when I repeated funny things she said. I think of it this way: She is going to laugh at what I say and how I dress someday, so now it's my turn. Going to Disney World to see "Mixie" and "Goosy" is better than going to see Mickey and Goofy. I feel confident she won't go to college saying those names wrong.

 Your children will laugh at you someday, so use the first few
Fumble *years to laugh at them.*

Kids would probably talk better if they weren't faced with an endless stream of adults talking baby talk to them. They mimic what they hear. And the more language they hear, the better. Of course, adults may delay their language development by being cute. Is it a dog, a doggy, a puppy, or a doggy woggy? My daughter took over a year to realize they were all the same thing.

During the first year is a great time to learn the best skill any QB dad can learn—listening to your kid. It seems silly to listen to that unintelligible babble escaping from her lips, but it is not. You are developing a trust in her. She will realize that you are going to care about what she says. That will become more important in the coming years, but now you are laying the ground work. NFL quarterbacks don't throw their first pass in the NFL. They have been passing footballs for years. Oh, besides listening, paying attention would also be a good idea.

Mastering Key Phrases

Because my star used to watch *SportsCenter* with me, she said "en fuego" at a young age. Lots of QB dads make an early goal for the baby to learn "Touchdown!" and the appropriate arm movements. A slightly easier goal would be for her to do the arm movements when you call touchdown. My daughter's first combination of words was "football game." She makes me proud. Of course, for the next twelve months she said "football game" for all football-related things. Helmets, players in pads, footballs, and actual football games all went by that title. That gave me a chance to explain the intricacies of my favorite sport. I hope by the time she is three she will be able to tell the difference between a 4-3 and a 3-4 defense.

Touchdown

All QB dads should shoot for "Touchdown!" and the appropriate arm signals by twelve months.

The baby may even start baby sentences during the tail end of the first year. Baby sentences are short two-word phrases that get straight to the point. Kids see no reason to bother themselves with complete sentences. An elementary teacher might not be thrilled, but parents love to hear them. *Football game, play chase,* and *eat hungry* are a few early ones my star mastered.

TALKING AND BRAINS

Talk to your pediatrician if you are worried about your child's language development. If you look at any traditional baby books, you will see they contain a monthly checklist of things your little genius should be able to do. You need to make sure that your little genius can do every item on the list. If your star can't do something, you might bear the brunt of the head coach's wrath. If she has a favorite baby book, peek ahead and make sure your star is up to speed. This may take extra practice with your star, but it may save you some grief. On a serious note, if your child lags in any area discuss this with your pediatrician. As always, go to as many well-child visits as possible.

Enjoy your star's newfound attempts at language. Talk to her, read to her, and explain all the many things you are doing as you change diapers, give her a bath, or tackle any other task that you would have never imagined yourself doing two years ago. Think of your star as an eager rookie quarterback, taking in all this knowledge for use later.

It's also important to read to your star at least once a day. Keep early books extremely short. They make an abundance of board books that are designed for babies. You probably got several as shower gifts. If your little one is awake in the morning before you leave, read her a book. A baby book will only take two minutes tops.

ADULT TALK

Both partners need some adult conversation during the week. I'm not talking dirty talk here, but most guys wouldn't argue with that either (from the head coach). I am talking about conversation with other adults wearing clothes. This will be an issue if one of you stays at home with the kid. If both of you work, the problem will most likely be taken care of. Of course, I have worked a few places where nobody acted like an adult.

Encourage the stay-at-home partner to get out for this conversation. Join a play group, go out for dinner with friends, play poker once a week—almost anything will do. If you're a stay-at-home dad, you may be the exception in many play groups. When a guy takes his star somewhere during the week, most people assume he has been downsized. But attitudes are shifting, and many people will think this is a refreshing twist on tradition.

If getting out is impossible, try to have an in-depth conversation at least once a week with the head coach that doesn't involve the baby or your work. Talk art, politics, movies, and, my favorite, football. My wife loves football, so this is possible. If your head coach doesn't love football, you may want to choose another topic that you both enjoy discussing.

Your star is becoming a little person, and guys are much more comfortable with little persons than babies. I have a friend that loves kids; he just wants them handed to him at four years of age. He wants a little buddy to do things with. I think you need to establish a basis for your relationship during this first year. The baby is much more aware of what is

BARKING OUT SIGNALS

What your star says:

> Hi Dad. Would you please get me a bottle?

What you hear:

> Goo Goo

Crying is the first form of communication for your star.

When babies talk, they know what they are trying to say.

Watch *SportsCenter* once a day for language skills.

How young a child talks is not an absolute measure of intelligence.

Talk to your star all the time you are around her.

Look ahead in baby books to coach your star on needed skills.

Once your star begins talking, he may never shut up.

going on than you think. Bonding during the first year is like a QB throwing extra balls to his receivers. It will benefit you more than you realize.

Touchdown

 Keep talking to your child all the time; she understands more than you realize.

In the first year, talk to your star and listen to him. The communication will help you get comfortable with having a little tailback to do things with. Your little star will develop into a little pal if you put the time in early, and it will help your little tailback in countless ways.

THE WHISTLE BLOWS ON YEAR ONE

You survived the first year; you are a veteran QB dad now. The joy and happiness of first seeing your number one draft pick is a distant memory. Could it really have only been one year since your life forever changed?

That year probably flew by. The sleep-deprived early months cause a chuckle when you think of them now. The happy memories of her sleeping on your chest while watching *SportsCenter* are just that: memories. Appreciate those memorable moments as you reflect back. So much has changed in that year.

PLANNING THE GREATEST PARTY EVER

You have to prepare for a celebration to celebrate the end of the first year. As the QB dad, you need to throw the best Super Bowl bash ever for her first birthday. Planning for the party is a shared responsibility. The head coach may try to do all the work, but try to help and guide her.

Fumble *Insist on a football-themed party for the first birthday party. Your star will decide in future years.*

You need to insist on a football theme. Super Bowl I needs to be memorable. Your star will insist on Clifford, Curious George, or the Wiggles in the future, but she won't care in year one. It won't matter if it is baseball or basketball season, football is year-round now. The head coach will need some persuading to allow this, but you have it in you. Promise her the moon if she will agree to this. Agree to let her plan the next ten years' worth of parties.

Decorations

Decorate the room with all types of football memorabilia. Clean out your game room for decorations. Crepe paper, balloons, and confetti in your team's colors are also available. You could even get a small Lombardi Trophy as a decoration. Plan ahead and buy football decorations during the buildup to the NFL's Super Bowl. There are plates, bowls, napkins, and helmet-shaped dip bowls available in January. Stock up.

Decorate with crepe paper. Crepe paper only exists for school dances and birthday parties. It is easy to put up and take down. To assist in taking it down, run all strands around the ceiling fan. After everyone leaves, turn the ceiling fan on and the room will be cleaned in no time.

 After the party, all helium must be sucked in by the QB **Fumble** *dad before singing your favorite song.*

After the party is over, all helium balloons must be deflated one at a time. Suck in the helium and sing all of your favorite tunes. Be sure to throw out all of the balloons, since they are a choking hazard for toddlers. Rap, country, rock, lullabies, and college fight songs all sound better under the influence of helium, and your little star will love it.

Party Food

Tailgate food is perfect for this wonderful occasion. Nachos, hot dogs, hamburgers, brats, and brews are all good choices. No beer for the birthday girl, of course. Every guy has one secret football recipe; this is a perfect chance to make this again. A football-themed cake can be ordered from almost any bakery. You could also easily make a football-shaped cake. Just use chocolate frosting for the base coat and decorate with white icing for the laces. Or you could make football cupcakes.

Give your star a miniature cake to eat. No forks are allowed. The photos that are created will be priceless. You might want to put an old tablecloth under the high chair. She will be on a sugar high for a while, but all the activity will wear her out. A friend of mine even created birthday cards using that cake-covered face on the outside of the card, which is a neat way to preserve and share the memories.

Touchdown

 Give your star a mini cake to eat alone. The pictures will be worth the mess.

If you can pull off the Super Bowl party you will be the envy of every QB dad in the neighborhood. My head coach vetoed that plan and we had a teddy bear theme instead. But

I have turned my daughter into a football fan, so I might get year number two (or three). I did buy all the decorations already, so I am ready.

Capturing the Moment

Regardless of what type of party you have, here are some hints. Keep the camcorder charged and running. You can edit out all of the boring stuff later. This is like recording a game; you can fast forward through the mundane stuff. Just like a game, sixty minutes of clock time becomes twenty minutes of useful footage. Editing tape is easier in the digital age, since you can download it into a computer and cut away. You can also add all sorts of neat bells and whistles using the computer. At least that is what I have been told; I am not at that level yet.

To record all the moments in your star's life, digital cameras are the way to go as they allow you to shoot away and trash the shots you don't like. Kids don't always smile when you want them to, at least until they turn five.

The head coach probably doesn't trust you to wrap presents. But if she does, wrap packages loosely so your star can open them easily. Most guys wrap packages this way already, so this won't be hard. Don't use the entire roll of tape (like you do at Christmas). You want the baby to be able to open it.

PLANNING FOR THE FUTURE

After the party you need to start planning for year two. As a QB dad, you need to train your kids early. Here are a few of the things you have to teach all kids. The remote control is daddy's. My daughter even calls it "Daddy's mote" and hands it to me. She also cries when the head coach has it. She will harass the head coach until it's returned to its rightful owner. Also, *SportsCenter* must be watched once each day before the channel can be turned.

Most experts agree on limiting television time for babies. The American Academy of Pediatrics recommends no television for the first two years and only one to two hours a day for older kids. There are educational shows on television, but the amount of time needs to be controlled. Set limits on the television, except for Saturdays and Sundays during football season. Watching games together is a bonding experience.

 Teach all children that the remote is daddy's.

Fumble

The next rule is that the star never eats in daddy's chair. Eating anywhere else is fine, but daddy's chair is a no-no. Sitting on spilled applesauce is not pleasant. The head coach may set other rules for where the little star can eat, and you should always try to keep the head coach happy. Daddy's beer is off limits, at least until your little star turns thirty.

All kids need to learn how to throw a perfect spiral by the end of year two. Practice with the little stuffed football that she already has. This skill may not be completely mastered by the end of year two, but you are well on your way. And also teach them to keep their head up when they tackle you. Good tackling form is important. When they tackle you on the living room floor, make sure they don't drop their head.

Sons have a few gender-specific things to learn. Sons need to be taught the one urinal rule for public restrooms. Trust me, the head coach will not teach this rule. It is an official guy secret; we must never tell women about this rule. Sons must also be taught to open doors, say "thank you" and "please," and our favorite fight song. And they need to be taught that you always ask mom for money. Sons are genetically engineered to control their moms.

Touchdown

Boys and girls are different and have different rules.

Daughters also have a few gender-specific things to learn. The most important thing is no dates until she turns twenty. Even at twenty, all dates must be approved by dad. Daughters must also be taught to say "please" and "thank you," and how to sing our college fight song. They also need to be taught that you always ask mom for money. This rule will not work for girls, but it is worth a try. She will ask and you'll give in, end of story. It has been that way for hundreds of years. Daughters have genetic code built into their DNA that allow them to own their dear old dads.

RULES FOR QB DADS

All QB dads must also learn a few rules. One rule is to talk to your kids all the time. Explain to them what you are doing even when it is boring. They will benefit from this as you teach them language skills. Also listen to them. They know what they are

CONCLUSION

THE WHISTLE BLOWS ON YEAR ONE

Planning the First Birthday Party

Friends, family, matching plates and hats

Can my star blow out candles wearing a football helmet?

Cake!!!!

EXTRA POINTS

Look back on the first year and enjoy the memories.

Laugh with the head coach about all of the silly moments.

Try for a football-themed party for the first birthday party.

Give your star a mini cake to eat and enjoy.

Continue teaching your star the rules for life.

Number one rule to teach: The remote is daddy's.

Teach your star how to throw a perfect spiral.

Look forward to many years of happiness.

saying even if you don't. When you listen, they will develop a trust in you. You want them to get used to talking to you.

Second rule is to learn a skill that will make you stand out from the other dads. This can be a skill that you already have acquired, but it needs to be somewhat unique. Throwing a perfect spiral, juggling, woodworking, hitting a softball, painting, singing, and playing a musical instrument are all good choices. Most of the tricks you learned in college are not going to be appropriate. My dad could talk like Donald Duck (and hit a softball a country mile). That gave me a leg up in playground arguments. Yeah, your dad may be taller, but mine can produce understandable quacks.

The first year probably flew by. You created a lifetime of memories, some funny and some nerve-wracking. As your star grows, enjoy the ride. Don't be afraid to hug, laugh, and cry with your star as the needs arise. Try to be an involved and active parent. Know who her friends are, who her teachers are, and what she likes to do for fun. Talk to your little star, even when he doesn't want to talk back. He will grow and change in the coming years, and communication is the key to staying in his life. Don't be afraid to be a parent to your little star. Most kids want structure in their life. You can be friends later in life. As your little star grows, she needs a parent more than another friend.

You only get one chance to raise your kids. That is the single most important thing you should remember. In a PE class it may have been okay, but there are no do-overs in raising kids. As one anonymous NFL player told me, "Close the laptop, turn off the television, look your kid in the eye, and listen to them." For more dad tips, go to *www.quarterbackdad.com*.

INDEX

ABOUT THE AUTHOR

Bobby Mercer has been a high-school physics teacher and football coach for almost twenty years in Orlando and Asheville. During the years coaching, he has experienced everything from a winless season to a perfect state championship season. As a teacher, he has won several awards for innovative, hands-on teaching strategies. He is the author of two juvenile science books: *Smash It! Crash It! Launch It!: 50 Mind-Blowing Eye-Popping Science Experiments* and *The Leaping, Sliding, Sprinting, Riding Science Book: 50 Super Sports Science Activities*. He lives outside of Asheville with his head coach and rookie of the year (*www.bobbymercerbooks.com*).